A Universe That Hopes

© 2024 ELLIS POTTER

Without limiting the rights under copyright reserved above, no part of this publication may be reproduced, stored in, or introduced into a retrieval system, or transmitted in any form or by any means (electronic, mechanical, photocopying, or otherwise), without the prior written permission from the publisher, except where permitted by law, and except in the case of brief quotations embodied in critical articles and reviews. For information, write: info@destineemedia.com

Reasonable care has been taken to trace original sources and copyright holders for any quotations appearing in this book. Should any attribution be found to be incorrect or incomplete, the publisher welcomes written documentation supporting correction for subsequent printing.

Published by: Destinée Media www.destineemedia.com

Cover design by Ben Stone
Cover and interior by Ben Stone
Formatting by Ben Stone
All rights reserved by the author.
ISBN 978-1-938367-83-0

Introduction

"A Universe That Hopes" is a trilogy of three books: "3 Theories of Everything", "How Do You Know That?" and "Comprehensive Spirituality". 3 Theories of Everything compares three different worldviews or ways of understanding reality. "How Do You Know That?" is about four fundamental ways of knowing or relating to reality: through the Bible, Rationality, Experience and Institutions. "Comprehensive Spirituality" is about having a unified or wholistic understanding of the unity of the natural and supernatural parts of reality.

The main point of the trilogy is that the whole universe, including people, hopes because everything was made by a Personal, Trinitarian God Who loves what He has made and said, "It is good". The trilogy is published in the hope that you, the reader, will have more true and realistic hope concerning your life and relationships.

For a long time I have wanted to see these three books together in one book. Many years ago my editor, Peco Gaskovski, shared this vision and suggested the title "A Universe that Hopes". May this trilogy be a blessing, an encouragement and a challenge to you who read it. God bless you.

Ellis Potter
Basel, 2024.

Table of Contents

3 Theories of Everything   7

How do You Know That?   123

Comprehensive Spirituality   217

3 THEORIES OF EVERYTHING

INTRODUCTION

THE FIRST CIRCLE
    The New Age Movement
    Experiencing Oneness
    The Cycle of Life
    Meditation and Language
    The Nothing of Zen

THE SECOND CIRCLE

THE THIRD CIRCLE
    The Problem of Opposites
    Humpty Dumpty

        Falling in Love on a Bridge
        Defying Gravity
        Change, Time, and Eternity
        Me and We
        You Gotta Serve Somebody
        Look, Daddy, Look!

        A Black Hole in the Heart
        The Solution
        To Put it Simply

45 QUESTIONS
    Themes for discussion
    with responses by Ellis Potter

○ ○ ○

WHEN I WAS A BOY I asked the kinds of questions that many children ask. Children want to know how far is far, how small is small. They especially want to know *why?* I never grew up. I am still asking these questions, absolute questions, about life itself. I want to know what reality looks like when you think down to the bottom and out to the edges. I want to know what things mean in the final and absolute context. It can be difficult to ponder absolute questions because they can challenge our deepest beliefs. They can be threatening. But it's exciting to ask absolute questions. I believe it's healthy. I hope that if any of you have grown up that you will go back to being a child.

Small children start off with the hope and trust that reality makes sense. They believe that Mommy and Daddy are omniscient—a belief that is smashed sometime in childhood. It turns out to be like Santa Claus. By the time they are adults, most people have lost their hope and trust about how everything fits together. Their concept of reality shrinks to a narrow cultural viewpoint, to self-protection and control, or to indifference. They live in a smaller reality because the big reality, the absolute reality, is too difficult.

An absolute is a category that is so big that everything fits inside and nothing is left over. The category of *absolute reality* includes everything in existence. It's a theory of everything. Many people think there aren't any absolutes and they say 'there are absolutely no absolutes.' There is, however, a problem with this statement, because if it's absolutely true, then it must be absolutely false.

I believe the existence of absolutes is most likely, but is inconvenient and disagreeable to our egos. People nowadays are often motivated *not* to believe in absolutes, because if there are true absolutes, then we are responsible to the absolute. If there are true absolutes outside ourselves, then we don't invent ourselves. On the other hand, if there are no absolutes, we are free. We invent ourselves, and the meaning of everything is our reaction to it. This idea is obviously quite attractive. It also means we can stop asking questions.

But some people keep asking. They want to know what life is really about. What does it all mean? They want the truth. They don't want to just 'fit in' with their culture or believe what their parents taught them. They want to know what is real and actual, and they don't care what it turns out to be like. If it's meaningless and dead, so be it. If it's purposeful and glorious, so be it. And so they keep asking questions right to the bottom and out to the edges of reality, hoping to reach the truth, the *absolute* Truth—whether there is hope in it or not.

The Three Circles

When I looked for absolutes, I discovered there weren't many. I believe it comes down to three: Monism, Dualism, and Trinitarianism. They are quite different, but they do have some things in common, not least of which is the suffix *-ism*. *-Ism* means that whatever comes in front of the suffix *-ism* is the center of reality and the measure of everything. If science is the measure of everything, you have *scientism*. If the human being is the measure of everything, you have *humanism*. In terms of worldviews, there is *one-ism*, *two-ism*, and *three-ism*.

The most important thing these three worldviews have in common is their view of the history of reality. They each understand that there was a perfect beginning and then something went wrong, so that we now live in a situation that is not the way it was intended to be. We suffer. We are alienated. We worry. We feel confused. We want things to be made right again. Is there anybody who has never complained about how things are in the world? Very few people believe everything is perfect in the world, and most of them are either pretending, deluded, or never read the news. I believe it's normal to complain about things because things are obviously not right. It's understandable that people want things to be made right again.

The Western tradition of thought recognizes that the idea 'things were once perfect and need to be made right again' is the biblical view of history. In the beginning, a perfect God made a perfect creation and perfect people, and then something went wrong. There was rebellion, sin, and egotism. As a result, things are not right and we suffer, and we look for things to be made right again in Christ. This movement expressed in abstract terms is:

perfect—imperfect—perfect

Or better yet:
home—away—home again

In other words, it's a pattern of homecoming, of being away on a journey and returning to the place where you started, usually in a transformed way. You see this pattern in great stories, such as Homer's *Odyssey*, and you hear it in most music, whether in simple folk songs or in the *aba* pattern of the Viennese sonata form. Music and stories are so powerful because they are microcosms of the basic structure of the universe.

Now, if we recognize that things are not right, an important question is: What was reality like when it was perfect? If we know the answer, then we can have a better idea of what is wrong and what we can do about it. If we don't know the answer, then we can only say 'Ouch, I hurt.' Do you remember René Descartes? Descartes said, 'I think, therefore I am.' But I prefer to say 'I *hurt*, therefore I am.' I think that's closer to our experience.

There's an apocryphal account about Descartes. He went into a bar one day and ordered a beer. After he finished the beer the bartender asked, 'Do you want another one?' Descartes replied, 'Oh, I think not,'—and he disappeared.

But I doubt we would vanish if we stopped thinking. We would still exist. We would still feel. We would continue to suffer. There are people in the world who actually seek out painful experiences so that they can feel alive. They cut themselves and pierce themselves with razors and needles because it makes them feel like they exist. This is not a good solution to the problem of suffering, but we can sympathize with the desperation and appreciate the hint of truth behind it. In an imperfect world being alive and feeling pain are interwoven. They are tied up like a knot. Is there any way to untie this knot? Is there such a thing as existence without pain? What is the solution to the problem of suffering?

Monism, Dualism, and Trinitarianism all agree that reality was perfect in the beginning, but they disagree about the nature of that perfection, the causes of suffering, and what it means to recover the original perfection. Each worldview, in other words, offers a unique solution, a unique hope, to the problem of suffering. We can represent Monism, Dualism, and Trinitarianism by showing a circle in three different ways.

THE FIRST CIRCLE

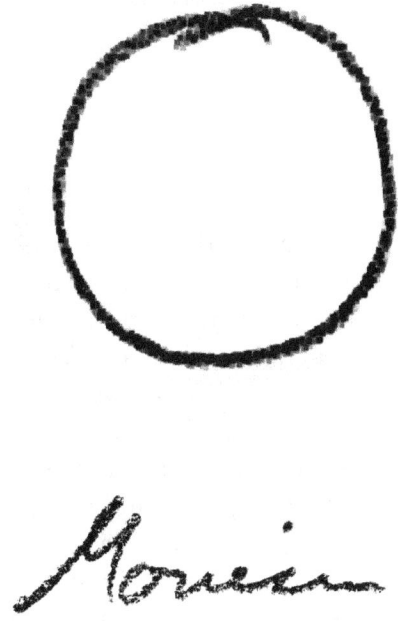

Monsieur

Let's begin with Monism. Monism is not the same as monotheism. Monotheism is the belief in one God, but Monism is the belief in one *One*, a total unity that is the ground of everything. That is very different. If you believe in one God, then you have God and *not* God, but if you believe in one *One*, then you have only unity, or *All is One*.

Monism is an ancient worldview. It probably came about when people looked around at the world and felt a strong sense of unity. There is one earth, one sky, one sun, one moon, one human race, one cycle of day and night, one cycle of four seasons. At the same time, people saw diversity. They saw differences. The unities they witnessed were stable and dependable, but the diversities they witnessed were unstable and undependable. Monism argues that the original perfection is a perfect, changeless, eternal unity. We suffer because we have forgotten this original unity and live in an illusion of diversity. This illusion may seem very real to us, but it's an illusion nevertheless. According to Monism, the solution to suffering is to remember and realize the perfect unity again.

Monism is a central idea behind the New Age movement. Have you heard of the New Age? It's actually getting a little old at this point. The New Age came into popular thought about fifty years ago, in the time of the hippies, and draws some of its inspiration from astrology. There are twelve houses in the astrological zodiac, and history moves from one house to another like the numbers around a clock. We are now moving from the Age of Pisces, symbolized by two fish moving in opposite directions, to the Age of Aquarius, the Water Bearer, where all things flow together. We are moving from the age of opposition to the age of flowing together, and when everything flows together there is an increase in peace and tolerance, and the realization that all is One.

All is One! is the bumper sticker of the New Age movement. It's the great sound bite, the great evangelistic cry. *All is One.* If all is One, then you are God. You are the sun and the moon and the Milky Way and the whole universe. If all is One, then when you drink from a cup of water, you are God putting God into God. 'All is One' is so attractive because if everything is one, no one is going to disagree with anyone, no one will fight, no one will misunderstand, and no one will be lonely. All problems are solved if everything is one. You might sort of like this idea. If all is one, however, then you are me, and that might not be so attractive. If everything is one, relationships are evil because you only have relationships when you have the illusion of diversity. If everything is one, hatred is evil because hatred is a relationship, and love is also evil because love is a relationship.

Some people are inclined to protest against this line of reasoning because they don't want to give up the idea of love or relationship. But Monism is an absolute worldview that encompasses everything, and so you can't pick and choose to keep some parts of reality diverse or separate. Everything is one. Nothing is left out, nothing is divided, and everything is absolutely unified.

The New Age Elephant

A popular New Age story that symbolizes the idea that *All is One* is the story of the elephant. The elephant is a symbol of absolute truth, and humans are represented as blind people trying to discover that truth by touching the elephant. To me, it makes sense that the story involves a truth-*elephant* rather than, say, a truth-*bunny rabbit*. A rabbit is something you can wrap your arms around. An elephant is too big; you can't contain it and know it. The absolute truth, in other words, is *bigger* than I am. It's also reasonable that the people are blind because we are all blind in some ways.

In the story, the first blind person finds the tail of the elephant and says, 'Ah, the elephant is like a rope.' The next blind person finds a leg and says, 'No, the elephant is like a tree.' The third blind person finds the nose and says, 'No, no, the elephant is like a hose.' The fourth one comes to the side and says, 'No, no, the elephant is like a wall.' There is only one elephant, but the people have very different experiences of the elephant.

The elephant is too big for them to embrace and experience in totality, so they are confronted with a choice. One choice is to believe in the validity of one's own experience of the elephant, and—believing that all the others are wrong—argue, fight, and kill each other. The other choice is to respect each other's faith journeys and realize that *all* experiences are experiences of the elephant, and so we should live together in peace and tolerance. Which is the better choice?

Maybe you feel caught. On the one hand, you don't want to say that everyone's concept of truth is equally true, but on the other hand you don't want to say that we should argue and fight and kill each other. Actually, I once told the story in the United States and a young man put up his hand and said, 'Kill each other.' There is a certain honest logic in this reaction, but most people (even most Americans) would not think it was the best solution.

You can see by the way the elephant story is framed that it leaves you stuck, with no real alternative but to agree with the conclusion that everybody has a little piece of the truth, and nobody's piece is any more valid than anybody else's piece. But is there anything wrong with the elephant? When I ask this question during my talks, people usually focus on problems with the blind people. They may point out that the people don't pool their experiences, or that they are blind, or that they are small. These might certainly be problems, but what about the elephant?

Notice that the people in the story are active and communicative, but the elephant is not. He is passive and silent. He is available, he doesn't hide, but he doesn't come to the people who are hungering to find out about him. You see, in the elephant story, the absolute truth—the elephant—is less complex than the particulars—the people. But is this reasonable? Is this what we would expect of the absolute truth? What do you think?

Another New Age story that expresses the idea that all is One involves a drop of water. A drop of water has many problems. It is lonely. It worries about evaporation. It is frustrated because the function of water is for fish to swim in, but the drop of water is too small for anybody to swim in. The solution to its problem is to go back into the ocean and to become one with the all. Then the drop of water laughs at evaporation and is never lonely and the fish swim in it. This is how enlightenment is taught to children.

Experiencing Oneness

The idea that all is One has its roots in ancient versions of Monism. It is the foundation of Hinduism and Buddhism, the great monistic religions. The founder of Buddhism was Siddhartha Gautama. He meditated under the Bo tree for forty days and forty nights, and then he was enlightened. He opened his eyes and saw the planet Venus on the horizon. He knew he was enlightened, because he knew he was looking at himself. If all is One, I am the planet Venus. If all is One, you are God.

When I was a teenager doing Yoga and Buddhist meditation I had an unforgettable experience one afternoon. I experienced being the exact same size as the entire universe. The experience lasted about fifteen minutes and was very intense, although it could not have been very transformative or else it would not have become a mere memory. For the deeply enlightened person this experience is a constant reality.

There are many different forms of Buddhism, and people in the Western world are generally fascinated by them. Often, however, I believe we learn the surface details about something like Buddhism without going down into the basic principles of it. I don't want to talk about the details here. I want to focus on the basic principles.

In Buddhism there are four spiritual laws, called *The Four Noble Truths*. The first noble truth is *the law of suffering*. The law of suffering is that everything suffers. Everybody, whether they are from the East or West, can agree with that.

The second noble truth is *the law of the cause of suffering*. The cause of suffering is desire. If you desire, you suffer. You are not at peace. Desire is caused by relationships. For instance, if I meet with you, if I speak with you, I desire that you will like me and understand me. But you might not. As a result, I suffer—maybe not terribly, but I do. But it's actually worse than that, because even if you *do* like me and *do* understand me, I will desire to keep being liked and keep being understood, and so I never really escape the desire or the suffering that it causes. According to Buddhism, every form of desire—whether to be liked, or to be rich, or to be smart, or to be beautiful—causes suffering.

The third noble truth is *the law of the stopping of suffering through the stopping of desire*. Let me give you an example of what this means. If I have a toothache, and I desire that the pain will stop, and it does not stop, I suffer. But if I have a toothache, and I do *not* desire that the pain will stop, and it does not stop, I do not suffer. I am free. You see, the pain is there, but if I realize that I *am* the pain, I don't suffer. My experience is not *I have pain*, but *Pain is*.

The fourth noble truth is an eight-step therapy program to accomplish the goal of stopping desire. The program has a special name, *the Eightfold Path*. Are you familiar with the twelve-step program of Alcoholics Anonymous for overcoming alcoholism? You may have heard of other step programs that lead to health and coping with various difficulties. The Eightfold Path that the Buddha came up with is probably the original step program. Notice also that *fold* is a better word than *step*. If you have steps, then you leave step one when you are on step two, but if you have folds, like folds in a piece of paper, your progress keeps adding and building on itself, until you have all eight folds.

The Eightfold Path begins with practical things, like the right way of seeing things, right thought or purpose, right action, right speech, right way of earning a living, right effort, right mindfulness, right concentration, and then it adds larger parts of reality like the supernatural, the awareness and consciousness, and then meditation and Buddha-consciousness. In her book, called *Three Ways of Asian Wisdom,* Nancy Wilson Ross describes the process like this: First, you must see clearly what is wrong. Then you must decide to be cured. Then you must act and speak so as to aim at being cured. Your livelihood must not interfere with your therapy. Your therapy must go forward steadily, as fast as possible, but not too fast. You must think about it constantly, and learn to contemplate with a deep mind.

The Cycle of Life

Realizing the absolute unity of all reality is a long process. Many people soon discover that it's not reasonable to expect that in your lifetime you would manage the whole process. At this point the doctrine of *reincarnation* becomes necessary. Reincarnation is the idea that after we die we are born into another life on earth, live again, die again, and then get reincarnated all over again. As we do, we work through our *karma*. Karma is like a law of cause and effect. Whatever we do in our lives produces effects that need to be re-balanced, and this re-balancing often occurs in another lifetime. For example, if we murder somebody in one lifetime, then in the next lifetime we ourselves might be murdered, or maybe we might devote ourselves to saving lives.

Reincarnation can go on for thousands of lifetimes. In the West we tend to regard it optimistically, maybe because we're positive by nature. We think, 'Ah, you get another chance! That's good! Maybe I'll be born a king next time!' But in Asia reincarnation is not regarded as a blessing. It's more like a curse to be born into a life of suffering over and over. The goal of Buddhism and also Hinduism is not to be reincarnated but to *stop* being reincarnated.

When a Christian tells Buddhists or Hindus that they need to be *born again* they will reply, 'Oh, I know—and again and again!' Being born again doesn't sound like good news to a Buddhist or Hindu.

There is a word that Buddhists and Hindus use to describe the illusion of reality. It is *maya*. Being caught in maya is like being stuck in a bad dream. The dream is painful, frightening and uncomfortable, but it's not real. What is the solution to a bad dream? You wake up. Awakening is the true realization of reality. It's also called *enlightenment*. It's waking from the nightmare of diversity and into the full realization of perfect unity. That is the gospel of Monism. That is the salvation of Monism. It's powerful, absolute, and deeply inviting. As a former Buddhist monk I can still appreciate this worldview and the strong attraction of it.

Meditation and Language

Methods are required to move toward salvation in Buddhism, Hinduism, and other Monist religions. The main method is called *meditation*. In the West, people sometimes think that meditation is concentrated thought. This is not what it means in the East. Rather, meditation is a method for the *stopping* of thought. Thinking must stop because thinking is analytic and relational. Thinking keeps us trapped in the web of maya, in the illusion of difference and diversity. It prevents us from realizing that if all is One then there are no relationships. There is only perfect unity.

Meditation doesn't have an agenda or logic about it. It is *being*. If you have a goal, you have a relationship with that goal. Meditation helps us not to have the goal but to *be* the goal. There are various ways of meditating, and many of them are quite therapeutic. If you follow various meditation practices regularly, you will feel more relaxed and focused, your stress levels will go down, your blood pressure will go down, the alpha waves in your brain will increase, your capacity to concentrate will increase, there will be more oxygen in your blood, your need for sleep may decrease, and you may live longer. Meditation is hard, but there are real benefits that come from it.

The people who practice it are not masochists. They are human beings like all other human beings. They want to be better and feel better. They want to make their lives better and healthier.

Aside from the practical benefits, the fundamental reason for practicing meditation is to achieve enlightenment. It takes many lifetimes to get to that point. Hinduism symbolizes the process of reincarnation as a wheel of birth and death that constantly turns—you are born into suffering and then you die, and then you are born into suffering and then you die. The purpose of meditation is to free yourself from the constant turning of this wheel.

Now, you don't become free by flying off the edge of the wheel, but by coming into the center. *Centering* is very important in meditation. Think about the center of a wheel or a car or bike. What is it? It is the axle. What is the center of the axle? It is a point. And what is a point? It is nothing. Even in physical reality, in the center of the center of the center, in between the molecules and atoms and gluons and electrons and protons, is nothing. This nothing does not turn with the wheel. The nothing is free from the turning. When you reach this absolute nothing through your meditation you also realize the absolute everything. You have achieved absolute freedom. You are fully enlightened. You become everything when you become nothing.

One of the most common methods of meditation is *mantra*. Mantra involves the repetition of words that have a meaning, first repeating them aloud and then internally. With enough repetition, they become a vibration and transcend their meaning. They become finer and finer until you are vibrating along with every atom in the universe. All physical matter vibrates as electrons change orbits. When you realize that vibration, you unite your self with all physical matter in the cosmos, and you become one with the all. This idea is where the New Age movement gets the concept of 'good vibes'. Good vibes are the vibrations of salvation, the vibrations of the unity in all reality. The use of mantra is not worship, even though religious words are sometimes chosen. Worship involves a relationship and functions in diversity. The goal of mantra is to be relieved of diversity and relationships and to realize the unity of all. For this reason, the goal of mantra meditation is to destroy language, because all language involves relationships among different things. You have to destroy language to be saved and to achieve total unity.

There are a variety of mantras. A simple one, and one of the most common, involves repetition of the word *AUM*. I remember chanting it in a monastery. When you do it, you breathe three times per minute. You empty your lungs completely and you fill them completely. When you really get going, there seems to be no motion. You don't know whether you're inhaling or exhaling. You don't know whether there is sound or silence. All becomes one.

When I give my talks, I usually perform one or two AUMs in order to give people an idea of what is sounds like. A philosophy professor once came to me afterward and said, 'I felt something inside of me when you did the AUM, something really big. I want to understand it.' I told him, 'You can't understand it. Understanding it means having a relationship with it, and that's not what AUM is about. AUM is about becoming one with AUM.'

The whole text is *aum mane padme hum*, which means *hail to the jewel in the lotus*. Lotus blossoms grow in the mud under the water, and propagate by shoots. Certain species have no seeds with a long stem and emerge through the surface of the water. If you see a statue of Buddha, look at the base and you will see little lotus blossom petals. It's the lotus throne, and he has lotus feet. It's a very important image for Buddhism. The lotus blossom has hundreds of petals. If you separate the petals and come into the center of the lotus blossom, what is there? Nothing. That is the jewel in the lotus. The imagery is beautiful and powerful. Buddhism may not be perfect, but it's not stupid or ugly.

A more complex mantra is *gate gate paragate parasamgate bodhi svaha*. The meaning is *gone, gone, gone beyond, gone beyond beyond, hail to the jewel in the lotus*. Repeat those words ten times every morning and your life will change. I can't tell you how it will change, but you will probably experience something. The poetry and symbolism are powerful. The words can still bring tears to my eyes when I hear them.

The Nothing of Zen

There are many kinds of Buddhism, such as Mahayana, Theravada, Tantric, Lamaistic, Nichiren Soshu, Pure Land School, and others. People from each kind of Buddhism will tell you 'our kind of Buddhism is the original true Buddhism.' We have the same situation in the West. There are many people who believe that God is a Lutheran, but we know He's a Baptist. Buddhists don't have problems that Christians don't have.

Earlier I said I am a former Buddhist monk, but actually I was a Zen Buddhist monk, and so I can tell you that Zen Buddhism *is* the original, true Buddhism. Zen really is special in some ways. The people who practice it believe in *Nothing*. They are not *Monists*, they are *Nonists*. But it's not a negative Nothing, it's a positive Nothing. Zen asks: If everything is reducible to One, then to what is the One reducible? This question is similar to the one posed by existential philosophers when they ask: Why is there anything? Why is there existence?

Zen doesn't answer the question with words and logical conclusions. It answers with an experiential realization. Let me try to give you some idea of the Nothing of Zen. You or I might say, 'It's possible that it will rain tonight.' This possibility is real and it's nothing.

You can't measure it, you can't weight it, you can't know what color it is. It is nothing. In the same way, everything that is—every object, every thought, every emotion, every action—is possible. God is possible, the devil is possible, the earth is possible, you and I are possible—and all of these possibilities are nothing. Possibility is the mother of everything.

Possibility, here, is not the same as probability. Probability is something you can describe and measure. Possibility is not. One of the deepest truths of Buddhism is *Buddha is possibility*. In Sanskrit we say he is *Tathata*, or suchness, or undifferentiated quality. The Shakyamuni Siddhartha Gautama is called the *Tathagata*, which means *the incarnation of undifferentiated quality*.

I used to study with a Zen master. He is now over one hundred years old and still teaching. He wrote one book called *Buddha is the Center of Gravity*. It's a fitting title for a book about Zen. Every object has a center of gravity. Your body, a truck, a boat, a building—everything. But can you describe the center of gravity? What color is it? What shape is it? How much does it weigh? The center of gravity can't be described in such terms because it's only a theoretical point. In that sense, it's nothing. But it is essential. You can think of the Buddha as the essential nothing—or, to say it differently, as the essential central pregnant nothing.

In Zen, we say: If you see the Buddha, kill him. That means *if you have an idea that absolute reality is outside of yourself, you have to get rid of that idea.* You see, you cannot have any idea of the Buddha. You can't think of him as the fat guy painted gold in the Chinese restaurant. You can't think of him as one of the standing Buddhas or sitting Buddhas or lying Buddhas either, and not as one of the skinny Buddhas or young or old Buddhas. You must not see the Buddha. You must *be* the Buddha. And you must not *become* the Buddha, because you always *are* the Buddha. You must awaken and realize Buddha-nature. Then there is salvation.

I have given you a short Buddhist sermon. I don't know if any of you will be converted. I hope that you can understand the power and hope that underlies this worldview, and why healthy, intelligent people would devote themselves to it. They are not crazy. There are many lovely people who are committed to this idea of reality.

THE SECOND CIRCLE

Not having really lived much in the second circle, I cannot truly give an insider's view of it. Although it has been very widely used as a theory of everything by many people in their thinking and believing, it is not as totally absolute as the first and third circles.

This circle, or at least a version of it, is known as the *umyang* in Korean. People from the West are usually more familiar with the Chinese terms *yin* and *yang*. Yin means *dark* and yang means *light,* and they symbolize the idea that absolute reality consists of opposites in harmony. You might also recognize this idea as connected with Taoism and Confucianism. It appears in other religions and philosophies as well, and is a good symbol for Dualism.

It's not hard to see how this view of reality may have come about. If we look around at the world, we observe many opposites in our experience of life: light–dark, hot–cold, hard–soft, pleasure–pain, sharp–dull, up–down, sweet–bitter, wet–dry, male–female. The idea behind Dualism is that life is good when opposites are in proper balance, or are in harmony with each other, but we suffer when there is imbalance or disharmony.

For example, if the weather is too dry, we suffer. If the weather is too wet, we suffer. If your personality is too outgoing, you suffer. If you are too withdrawn, you suffer. If we suffer because of imbalances, then the way of salvation, according to the second circle, is to restore the balance. The original perfection is a perfect balance or harmony of equal opposites.

Over the course of its history, the Dualist worldview has produced a number of therapies and practices to help accomplish balance in different areas of life, such as behavior, family and society, and past and present. The worship of ancestors is an example of the latter. Harmony is accomplished when living people, who exist in the present, give respect to dead people, who existed in the past. The same harmony can be accomplished when young people, who live more exclusively in the present, give respect to old people, who live more in the past. Also, younger people are stronger than older people, and the balance between the two is again brought into effect by respect—the stronger gives respect to the weaker. This kind of strategy may not always work out perfectly, but it can bring order to society.

Dualism has also influenced approaches to architecture and interior design through a system of aesthetics known as *feng shui*. To bring harmony to your living room, you might have a darker carpet to encourage yin energy, and bright walls to encourage yang energy. The overall result would be a balance of opposing energies and greater well-being to the people who spend time in that room.

Most of the strategies and therapeutic techniques of the second circle are probably effective to some extent. They make life better. They reduce suffering. They also produce different approaches in the case of health problems. In the West, our healthcare is typically based on pharmacology and surgery. This form of treatment is usually *against* something—against fever, against infection, against tumors, and so forth. In the East healthcare is often dietary and environmental and tries to bring the various elements in our body and its environment into harmony and balance with each other. Western healthcare concentrates on problem solving. Eastern healthcare concentrates on problem prevention. Both approaches to health can be effective—people from Asia don't live shorter lives or less healthy lives than people in the West—although sometimes the methods used in the East may seem strange or dubious to people who are not familiar with them. It might be good to combine the wisdom of East and West in some ways, although there is often a lot of distrust between people of different worldviews.

For a short while in 1975 I was involved with a macrobiotic community near Boston. This community was devoted to finding health and well-being through eating a balance of yin and yang foods. The yin side of things includes soft, dark, sweet, kind, and female. The yang side is hard, light, bitter, strict, and male. Most people's diet is much too yin with an emphasis on sugar, fat, cream, and alcohol. To bring balance one needs to eat yang foods, like short-grain brown rice, black radishes, green leaves, and seaweed. Somehow I was always afraid of showing up to a meeting with hot fudge sundae on my breath. People there told me that their founder became ill when he was old. After thinking through the possibilities for a long time he concluded that his system was too yang, which no one had ever heard of. So he basically went on a short diet of whiskey and ice cream, which seemed to help. We do need to work with the unexpected and surprising things in life rather than deny them.

Dualistic thinking has had a great influence on art, culture, philosophy, and politics. We can think of the dualistic basis of the Hegelian/Marxist dialectic with its thesis and antithesis, which engage dynamically through revolution and move toward the end, or synthesis, of Communism. These ideas were tried over several decades on a very large scale but finally proved to be unworkable at the end of the twentieth century. It seems to me that Communism is very religious in the sense that it requires faith in the vision of the prophet (Marx, Lenin, Mao, Stalin). Only through the priestly or prophetic vision of the prophet can we know what direction the dynamism of the revolution will take. The visions of the Communist prophets turned out not to fit reality.

There are many artistic examples of the Dualist worldview. One of the best known in film is the *Star Wars* series. *Stars Wars* involves a conflict between the forces of light, symbolized in the original movies by Luke Skywalker, and the forces of darkness, symbolized by Darth Vader. The solution and resolution of the tension between these two opposing elements is the Force, or a universal energy that is the source of everything and includes both a light and a dark side. There is, however, a problem with regarding the Force as totally unifying because light eventually triumphs over darkness in the *Star Wars* films. In other words, although the worldview of the films is Dualist, the conclusion is non-Dualist.

Although Dualism has been pervasive throughout our history, and has resulted in some practical applications involving health and living with balance, there are some difficulties with the second circle. One problem is that it doesn't really seem to be absolute. What is the opposite of a river? A desert is very different from a river, but is it the opposite? What is the opposite of time? Is it time running backwards? Is it eternity? There are many differences but not everything has a clear opposite. Somehow this absolute may not really be an absolute. It leaves some things out and so I begin to question Dualism as an adequate theory of everything.

Another difficulty is that, if the second circle is really absolute, then it has to include everything. It has to include both kindness and cruelty, and good and evil. If good and evil have to be brought into balance, however, then you can never have victory, because as soon as you have victory you have imbalance. The goal is harmony, not victory.

The Western tradition has long held that good and evil are not equal opposites. In the beginning there was good, and in the original context of good there came to be evil. In this view, evil cannot exist without goodness, but goodness can exist without evil. Most people hope that good overcomes evil, that kindness overcomes cruelty, that love overcomes hate. But the Dualist worldview doesn't allow for that.

A final problem with the second circle is that the harmony of opposites, if it's truly perfect and absolute, must be static. Nothing moves. If anything moves, the perfection is destroyed. When it's perfect it's absolutely still, and when it's absolutely still it's basically Monism—it's a unity. The second circle turns out to be the first circle rather than a totally distinct and separate worldview.

… THE THIRD CIRCLE

Trinitarianism

We can explore the third circle, Trinitarianism, using two approaches. The first approach involves looking around at everyday reality and asking: What could be the cause of this reality? The second approach involves using one of the basic sources of the Western worldview, the Bible, in order to see what it says about reality.

The first approach is called *natural* theology. It includes the kinds of things we learn through everyday observation and science. The second approach is called *revealed* theology. Revealed theology tells us things about reality that we could not figure out based on everyday observation and science.

Unfortunately, the two approaches, natural and revealed theology, are often seen as being in competition with each other. There are people on one extreme who insist that you can only understand reality through human observation and systematic reasoning, and people on the other extreme who are deeply suspicious of science and depend almost exclusively on the Bible. Understood rightly, I believe that the two approaches complement each other. Together they help enrich our view of reality, and for this reason I will make use of both of them in exploring the third circle.

The Problem of Opposites

According to the third circle, when we look around at the world we see both unity and diversity. In this way we are like the people of the first circle. But whereas the people of the first circle conclude that unity is good and diversity is not, and that unity is real and diversity is illusion, people of the third circle have a different view. They regard the original perfection, which is called God, as both perfectly unified and perfectly diversified.

We see a clear description of this reality in the Bible. God is perfectly unified as one God, and yet God is perfectly diversified in the three persons of the Father, Son, and Holy Spirit. There is unity and diversity in absolute reality. There is not one God who chooses to reveal Himself in three ways in order to create the appearance of diversity, and there are not three persons who choose to unite and cooperate in order to create the appearance of being unified. The original reality is 100% unified and 100% diversified. It's a 200% reality that cannot be comprehended by simple logic.

Here is a proverb I made up to capture the essence of this reality: *God alone is God, and God is not alone.* You cannot make this statement about any other God or original perfection. You can say *Buddha alone is*

Buddha, but that is all. The rest is silence. You can say *Krishna alone is Krishna* and *Allah alone is Allah*, but the rest again is silence. If the God of the third circle wants to talk to somebody, He talks among Himself, because He is three persons. A God who wasn't diversified could not talk among Himself. He would have to create something else to talk with. He would require a creation in order to be personal, whereas the God of the third circle is intrinsically personal, independent of His creation. His creation does not complete Him but rather expresses Him.

If the original perfection is both unified and diversified, it means that when we experience unity in reality it shouldn't be a problem, and when we experience diversity in reality it shouldn't be a problem. In other words, unlike Monism, the third circle does not regard diversity as the cause of suffering, and does not see the solution to suffering as involving a detachment from diversity. Also, unlike Dualism, the third circle does not attempt to resolve suffering by balancing opposites. Instead, the third circle sees variation and contrast as a part of the original perfection, and therefore, as a normal part of reality itself.

Along with unity and diversity, there are other ways in which God's creation represents a 200% reality. For example, one of the images of reality described in the Bible is marriage. We see this reality at the start of the Bible in Genesis, when God brings Adam and Eve together, and we see it again at the end of the Bible in the marriage supper of the Lamb in the Book of Revelation. Now, is marriage more male or female? Most people would say it's equal. Does that mean it's 50–50? No, because if you take away the woman you don't have half of a marriage left. You have nothing. Marriage is 100% woman and 100% man. It's a new reality, a 200% reality that includes dimensionality and mystery.

That may seem odd, but the ancient Hebrews thought differently from the people of the European Enlightenment and most people today. We tend to think of reality in terms of flat pie charts where the whole can be divided up into separate parts that add up to 100%. We may divide this reality into unity and diversity, or we may divide it in terms of other 'difficult' opposites such as objectivity and subjectivity, or predestination and free will. But a flat pie chart will never give us a stable solution to these kinds of opposites. For example, in the case of predestination and free will, does God choose me or do I choose God? I could divide up the pie chart 50%–50%, but it doesn't seem like I should be equal to God, and so maybe I should make it 51% God and 49% me? Then again, maybe it should be 99% God and 1% me, or maybe 100% God and 0% me, or maybe 100% me and God is on a deistic holiday? None of this, of course, is satisfactory. The pie chart won't work. The third circle regards God as 100% sovereign and people as 100% responsible. God's sovereignty and the free will of people are both fully real. In this mysterious complementarity, Calvin and Arminius kiss each other.

Another way to think about the third circle is in terms of physical dimensions. Think of God's sovereignty as 100% of a two-dimensional plane and think of free will as 100% of another two-dimensional plane. If you intersect these two flat disks, as in the image below, you create a third dimension that includes both elements within a three-dimensional complementary reality.

Within this intersection there is no competition or contradiction of opposites. They fit together in a single and complementary reality. I think it's fitting that a God consisting of three persons should create a reality that has at least three dimensions.

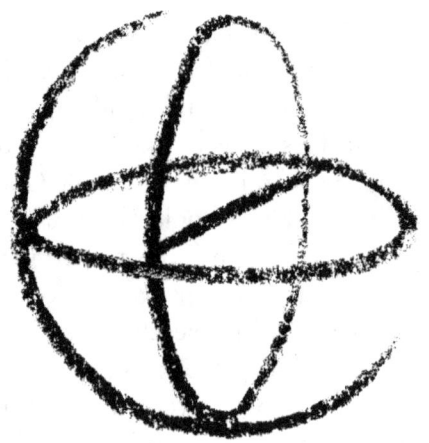

Humpty Dumpty

If you find the idea of dimensions too dry and geometric, we can also express things in terms of *Humpty Dumpty*. Do you know Humpty Dumpty? He was an English egg. I don't know if he was a good egg or a bad egg, but he was certainly a profound egg. Humpty Dumpty represents everybody. The nursery rhyme tells us that Humpty Dumpty sat on a wall. There are two sides to a wall. There is the objective side and the subjective side. There is the predestination side and the free-will side, and many other opposites that make up reality. Humpty Dumpty fell off the wall, but which side did he fall on? The objective side or the subjective side? The predestination side or the free-will side? We do not know. It doesn't matter. He fell, and if you fall on either side of those divisions it's disastrous because you need both sides to have reality. When you fall on one side you are dead because you have only half of reality.

So, Humpty Dumpty fell—there he was, poor egg, shattered and splattered on the ground.

Remember how the poem goes?

> Humpty Dumpty sat on a wall
> Humpty Dumpty had a great fall
> All the King's horses and all the King's men
> Couldn't put Humpty together again.

Good night children! Sweet dreams! We laugh but it's awful, isn't it? Many nursery rhymes are grim probably because the lives of children can be so hard. These little songs are quite profound. According to the third circle, however, the *Humpty Dumpty* rhyme is missing a line. A fifth line belongs to the poem, a line that will transform it into a glorious and hopeful poem. The line is this:

> But the King could.

The King's horses and King's men couldn't do it, but the King could. The pastors and the missionaries and the evangelists and the scientists couldn't do it, but the King could. The King is the God of the third circle. He is the solution to the cause of suffering.

So how exactly does He do it?

Falling in Love on a Bridge

Before we can fully understand the solution to the cause of suffering, we need to go deeper into the third circle. Let's explore objectivity and subjectivity a little further, because they are such common ideas in everyday reality. People have argued for centuries over which one is more true. Throughout European history, scientists (especially those of the Enlightenment) have believed in objective truth, and artists have believed in subjective truth. Nowadays, modernists believe in objective truth, and postmodernists gravitate to a more subjective truth.

As I have already suggested, however, the objective and subjective cannot really be divided from each other. Consider a desk. When I look at my desk, I see four legs, and I see a certain size and shape. When you look at my desk, you will likely agree on the size and shape, and on the number of legs, unless you look from a different point of view and only see three or two legs. If we each took a ruler, and we each measured the different parts of the desk, our measurements (assuming we were alert and careful) would agree exactly. But each of us also sees the desk subjectively. When I see my desk, I see the desk of my high school chemistry teacher, and I see the teacher himself, Mr. Corbett, standing beside it. But you wouldn't see him. You couldn't. In the presence of my desk, my seeing four legs and Mr. Corbett is a part of reality. My perception and my memories are not objective, but they are true—not objectively true, but subjectively true. They are not false.

We often argue over which half of reality is true. I do not believe in objective truth, but I also don't believe in subjective truth. I believe all truth is both objective and subjective. Another way of saying this is that we have accurate truth, which is objective, and we have non-accurate truth, which is subjective. The two belong together in a complementary manner in reality. If you want to build a bridge, you have to approach it objectively by making accurate physical measurements at every step of the process. If you do so, then, in the end, you will have a true bridge. But you cannot fall in love accurately. The process is chaotic. But a relationship of love is not false. Nor is it objective. The objectivity of the bridge is the same for everybody, but the subjectivity of falling in love is unique and exclusive. A complete experience of truth might be falling in love on a bridge.

In a similar way, the Bible includes two kinds of truth. One is accurate truth, the other is non-accurate truth. When the Bible gives us historical facts they are accurate truth. You can test them and do research about them. The parables of Jesus, however, are not accurate. You cannot research the name of the prodigal son because he never existed as a fact. The parables are not accurately true but they are profoundly true as windows and doors of subjective perception into reality. People can come to the truth of the parables uniquely from any point of view or set of circumstances.

Another way of expressing a full concept of truth is to say: Fact plus meaning equals Truth. Fact is objective, and meaning is subjective. When I work with students on various topics they often ask me, 'What does that mean?' I make their eyes roll when I ask them, 'What does *meaning* mean?'

In the most basic sense, *meaning* means relationships. There is fact, and there is the relationship of that fact to other facts, and that relationship is meaning. A fact has no meaning in isolation. The color red has no meaning in itself. It only has meaning in its relationship with blue or green or yellow. In the same way, you have no meaning in yourself but only in your relationship with your environment and other people.

Adam, according to the biblical account of creation, had no meaning in himself. When God made Adam, He said: *It is not good for man to be alone.* Adam was only a fact, only objective, because his was the only point of view within the creation. True subjectivity requires more than one viewpoint. God made Eve, and then it was good. There was subjectivity in the creation—just as there is in the Creator—as a result of relationship.

We see the same expression of meaning in God. In the original perfection of the third circle you have three persons, and the persons have no meaning in themselves.

The meaning of Jesus is not in Jesus. The meaning of Jesus is in His relationship with the Father and the Holy Spirit. The same is true of the other two—their meaning is in their relationship with each of the others. They also see each other from a different point of view. The Son, for instance, sees the Father from a different point of view than the Holy Spirit does. What they see is slightly different from each other, but they each see perfectly. These differences are a great liberation. It means we don't have to be clones of each other. We don't have to have the same taste. There can be true variety of point of view and reaction. Difference of perspective is a part of absolute reality, of the original perfection.

When we find out that the original perfection is like this—a true God who is both objective and subjective—then we shouldn't be surprised to experience objectivity and subjectivity in our reality. Nor should we think that one of them is the cause of suffering. But we often do. An artistic person may think that objective truth has no freedom and is the cause of suffering. A scientist may argue that subjectivity has no stable or reliable form and is the cause of suffering. The Bible describes an absolute truth that is objectively one God and subjectively three persons. Objectivity and subjectivity belong to each other in reality. Their relationship is not competitive but complementary.

Defying Gravity

Freedom and form is another pair of opposites that we see in the world. A good illustration is gravity. Gravity is one of the basic forms, or structures, of reality, but it gives us a certain freedom. If gravity were not here and I began to walk, I would float and spin and soon I would be dead. Form, or structure, is necessary. Let me give you an equation to express this idea:

$$total\ freedom = death$$

There is nothing postmodern about this equation. Postmodernism, as usually understood and practiced in Western culture, regards freedom as the highest value, and sees the purpose of freedom as fun and play. But freedom cannot really be valuable or life-giving unless it is accompanied by form. If you want to be totally free to fly, you can go to the top of a building and jump. You can say, 'I am free!' But you won't be free, you will be dead, because you have not respected form. But if you study the various forms of reality—the laws and properties that give reality structure and shape, such as gravity, aerodynamics, thermodynamics, metallurgy, jet propulsion, stress, torque, and so on—then you will be able to build an airplane and fly across the ocean. That's a great freedom, but the freedom is completely connected to form. Freedom and form are not independent of each other in reality. Again, their relationship is complementary rather than competitive.

What about God? The three persons of God give Him particular forms. The persons do not have the same form as each other. The form of the Father is to command and to send. The form of the Son is to obey and to go. Their forms are opposite in some ways, but they are both God. The form of the Holy Spirit is to hover over creation, to blow as a wind, and to indwell, teach and empower human beings. When each of these persons is faithful to His form, He is also free to be God. But if any of them were not faithful to His form then the creation would be destroyed, because the creation is dependent on the form of the Creator. If the Creator is unfaithful to His own character, the foundation is no longer there. The freedom and the form of God are both eternal. They must both be constant by His constant choosing.

For this reason, God is not automatic in being the way He is. He chooses to be faithful to His forms, and it costs something. The clearest way to see this cost is in the Garden of Gethsemane. Jesus, in staying faithful to the form of His promise, has come into creation in order to die for it and therefore to save it. The moment is coming to do that, and He realizes He doesn't want to. He prays to the Father, saying, *Please, if it can be any other way, let it be.* As He prays, the blood comes out of His skin and runs down onto the ground. He is experiencing intense stress. What does this mean?

It means He is struggling. He is not automatic. He is God, working, serving, giving, praying, in order to be Himself, for Himself and for us. There is no other God like that.

If form and freedom are a part of the original perfection, then they are not the cause of suffering. In other words, although we may suffer in the context of varying degrees of freedom in life, or varying degrees of form, we will not find salvation by simply getting rid of all forms or structures or by focusing only on freedom and possibilities. We need both form and freedom in our lives, because they are a part of the original perfection.

Change, Time, and Eternity

Dynamism is another aspect of the third circle. Dynamism means that things are not static. They change in relationship to each other. Reality involves before and during and after. In the first letter of Peter, we are told that before the world was made, the Son was chosen by the Father to come into the world and save it. In other words—before there was space and time—there was before the choosing, during the choosing, and after the choosing.

Dynamism occurs in two matrixes of sequence. I mean *matrix* in the same sense as in the movie *The Matrix*—an environment or context in which things happen. Water is the matrix of tea, meaning that tea happens in water. Cyberspace is the matrix of e-mail, meaning that e-mail happens in cyberspace. The matrix of sequence *in space* is time, meaning that everything that happens happens in time. The matrix of sequence *outside of space* is eternity. Many people think that eternity is infinite time, but that isn't how the Bible describes it. Eternity is a separate matrix of sequence in that every point of time is present to every point of eternity. That is why prophecy is possible. God lives in eternity, and from every point of the dynamic matrix of eternity, all of time is present.

This vision of absolute reality is different from what we see in Monism and Dualism. Monism regards dynamism as illusory and unreal. Dualism regards the original perfection as the harmony of opposites, which, if absolute and perfect, must be static and without any change. In the Zen view, you would say *I enter the water and I make no ripples, because everything is always the same.* There is no motion.

The third circle sees dynamism as a real and non-illusory part of absolute reality. God is dynamic and His creation is dynamic. For this reason, dynamism cannot be regarded as the cause of suffering.

Me and We

Another major element of the third circle, and one that Christians like to emphasize, is that God is a *personal* God. I couldn't agree more with this statement. But God is not a personal God because I personally believe in Him. He is not a personal God because I have a personal relationship with Him. God was a personal God before I was born. That He is personal is completely independent of creation, and stems from there being three persons in relationship with each other.

In this respect, God's nature tells us something about how we need to understand personality. Most psychological models present personality as a description of the individual. The same model has been adopted by the modern church, which sometimes defines people in terms of body, soul, and spirit. The problem with this idea is that it's all about the individual, whereas the biblical description of the person places primary emphasis on relationship. You see this reality in God's own nature, as separate persons in relationship, and you see it in the beginning of creation, when God created people in His own image. When Adam was still alone—when he was self-aware, and aware of his environment and of naming the animals—he was still not personal because he didn't have any relationships within the creation. He could relate to God outside of the creation but within the creation the image of God was not complete until it was *we* or *us* rather than *I* or *me*. The image of God is *we* based on relationships. Also, in a right relationship of man and woman as God originally designed it, there is a third person—a child. God is three persons and His image comes in sets of three persons.

The emphasis on relationship does not mean that the individual does not matter, or that individual identity is somehow lost. Individuality is completely retained but understood first and foremost in the context of relationship. Personality is self-aware consciousness in relationship with other self-aware consciousness. It can be difficult to accept this view of the person. It seems to put things in the wrong order. Many of us would prefer to define ourselves first by our identity and personal characteristics and second by our relationships. In the opening lines of the Gospel of John, we are told:

In the beginning was the Word, and the Word was…
How does the verse end?

People who don't know the verse expect it to say:
…*and the Word was God.*

But it doesn't say that. It says:
…*and the Word was with God, and the Word was God.*

Relationship comes first, then identity.
Relationship precedes identity.

You Gotta Serve Somebody

If relationship is a part of absolute reality, then it cannot be the cause of suffering. Relationship also brings with it a number of other elements. One of them is hierarchy. Hierarchy refers to relationships of authority. It means that some individuals have authority under certain circumstances—have the power and responsibility to describe reality—while other people are under authority. In our culture hierarchy feels wrong. It's politically incorrect. From a biblical perspective, however, hierarchy is a part of God's nature, and so it must be a part of reality itself.

An example of hierarchy is the relationship between parents and children. Parents have authority over small children. They have authority to describe bedtime and diet, and to describe play in the garden rather than in the street. Small children need this authority to describe reality for them in order to survive. They cannot adequately describe reality for themselves. Now, who is more human in this relationship, the parents or the children? You will say, of course, that they are equally human. But in other relationships you might hesitate. If you have a boss and an employee, who is more human? If you have beautiful, successful people on the one hand, and ugly failures on the other, who is more human? If you have rich people and poor people, who is more human? We get confused by this. We think that in hierarchical relationships, some people are more real or more valuable than others. This idea, however, belongs to the culture of a fallen world. It belongs to the church of a fallen world. It isn't the idea God wants us to have.

Hierarchy does not imply inequality of value or significance. In God, the Father commands and the Son obeys, and they are equally God. The Son is not an apprentice god waiting to get His certificate. He is not a junior god waiting to graduate. He is fully and eternally God, and He obeys. This view of God doesn't fit with our current culture because we think we are more human and alive when we command and less human when we obey. That can't be true if we're made in the image of God. To obey is equally divine as to command, and so to obey is equally human as to command. Hierarchy and authority are grossly misused, unfortunately, and this misuse causes great suffering. If hierarchy is a part of God, however, then it cannot in itself be the cause of suffering. Bob Dylan gets it right when he says *you gotta serve somebody*.

The Bible describes five basic relationships of authority. These are husbands and wives, parents and children, masters and slaves (or employers and employees in contemporary terms), the state and citizens, and elders and members of churches. That covers most of the major hierarchies of life. God, according to the Bible, has given us those relationships, and those relationships are good.

But they also malfunction. We experience suffering in all of those relationships. They don't work right. Sometimes, when we see that a relationship doesn't work right, we think that the solution is to eliminate the relationship. In the Western world, we find that marriage is problematic. Many people believe they can solve the problem by not having marriage. But I don't think that's going to be a solution, because that relationship is given by God.

It doesn't help to pretend that marriage is perfect. Marriage takes work in order to create a relationship of love and support. We must also be careful not to assume that the husband, who has authority, is more valuable and real than the wife. We must not assume that having authority justifies the abuse of power. The Bible doesn't give us that picture. C. S. Lewis wrote a book called *The Four Loves*, and one of the things he tells us is that the husband and father in a family should wear a crown, but it should be a crown of thorns. I think that's a good picture. He wears a crown and he is bleeding. He suffers. He carries the weight. That's an interesting balance, isn't it? If we look in the Bible itself, we hear Paul teaching us that the husband is to be like Christ to the wife, which means he should die to make her beautiful. That's an extreme picture. That's not politically correct. That does not fit in our world. It sounds ridiculous. But it's what the Bible gives us. There is a conflict between what the Bible gives us and the world we live in, and we need to think about and struggle with the conflict to find the right way.

Look, Daddy, Look!

Another aspect of relationship, and of the third circle in general, is needs. We all experience needs. We need to eat and drink and be warm and to live under a roof, but more deeply than that we need to be seen. You see it with small children. All day children will cry, 'Look, Daddy, look!' If it's a choice between eating lunch or Daddy-looking, getting Daddy's attention always wins because it's a more basic need. To be seen by Daddy or Mommy or other people that matter is more important than eating. And if Daddy and Mommy don't look because they're at work all the time or divorced or drunk or in jail or dead, or always on a missionary trip, then the need is not met and the child is horribly distorted and will suffer. That describes all of us.

We also need to be heard. Even before a child masters language, they coo and babble, making noises to be heard. It's painful for children when they are not heard. As adults we still need people to hear us when we speak, even if they disagree. It's deeply frustrating not to be heard. It diminishes our humanness.

We also need to make a difference. We need to have an effect on the world. If a child takes some blocks and piles them on top of each other, they're not the same as before.

They're different. *I did that* the child can say—and then the child knocks it down. Different again. Sometimes the child's need is not convenient, like when he or she smears lipstick on the wall, but you can still see the need to make a difference. It goes on through our entire lives. If we bake bread we need people to eat it. If we build a house people should live in it. Where I have been and lived and worked should not be the same as if I had not been there. This is how God made us to be.

Related to all of these needs is the need to be wanted. We need people to say 'Come, be with me, be with us, you are wanted.'

Why do we have these needs? Is it the result of sin? Do they come from the devil? Are these needs a temptation? You might say we have these needs because we are only human, but who defines what it means to be a human? According to the third circle, human beings are made in God's image. Their needs come from God because God has these needs. Maybe you have never thought about God having needs? It's not that God needs anything from *us*. Rather, He has needs among Himself, and exactly the same needs we have—to be seen, to be heard, to make a difference, and to be wanted. But God does not suffer from these needs. Having these needs is pure joy for God, because needs are the basis for trust and love. A need that can only be fulfilled by another person requires that you trust that person to fulfill it. If there were no needs, there would be no real trust or love.

Before there was any creation, when there was only God, there was already trust and love in reality because there was already a fulfillment of the need to be seen and be heard and make a difference and be wanted. Each of the three persons of God fills the needs of the other persons, and does so by emptying Himself for the others. Jesus empties Himself for the Father and the Holy Spirit. For this reason, the center of reality for Jesus is not in Jesus, it's in the Father and Holy Spirit. Each of the persons of God is similarly other-centered rather than centered in Himself. Such is the Bible's depiction of absolute reality: a totally other-centered God. This other-centeredness is the source of God's energy, for as each of the persons of God empties Himself once, He is filled twice by the others. This energy increases exponentially. It became so great that God could say *Let there be light!* and a universe was born. The Bible gives a name to this energy when it says *God is love*. It is an other-centered emptying and filling, a perpetual building up of energy. It is the energy of life. It is the foundation of all reality.

Notice that the Bible doesn't only say *God is loving* or *He loves*, although these are true. It's far more radical—God *is* love. Notice also that it says *God is just* but it doesn't say 'God is justice' because He's also merciful. And it doesn't say 'God is mercy' because He's also just. But when it says *God is love* it doesn't contrast that with anything. Love is the total reality of what God is.

Just as God is fully other-centered, we too were meant to be this way. When Adam was alone within the creation, God saw that it was not good, and so He made Eve. Now the identity of Adam could be fully outside of himself in relationship. The center of Adam was not in Adam; it was in Eve and it was in God. The center of Eve was not in Eve; it was in God and in Adam. The creation reflected the Creator. It's for this reason that we, like God, continue to have needs, and it's for this reason that we yearn for these needs to be fulfilled within relationships of love and trust with each other and with God.

If needs are a part of the original perfection, then they cannot be the cause of suffering. We may indeed suffer when our needs are not met, but the needs themselves are not the fundamental reason why things are not right in the world.

Up to now, along with needs, we have considered unity and diversity, objectivity and subjectivity, predestination and free will, form and freedom, dynamism, personality and relationships, and hierarchy—and *none of them*, according to the third circle, is the real cause of suffering in our world.

So what is? And what is the solution?

A Black Hole in the Heart

In the book of Genesis, we're told that God put the Tree of the Knowledge of Good and Evil in the Garden with Adam and Eve. And God said: *Do not eat the fruit of this tree. You must not know good and evil for yourselves. You must trust Me to tell you.*

You might wonder why God gave them the option of eating the fruit. Why not prevent them from doing it? Why not put a barbed wire fence around the tree? The reason, as I mentioned earlier, is that God is not automatic, and so His creation cannot be automatic either. Just as God is free to choose, and He chooses always to be faithful to Himself, we as the image of God are given the same choice—the choice to be trusting and dependent upon Him. So the possibility exists that we can choose wrongly.

I ought to point out that if God is non-automatic, then the possibility also exists that *He* can choose wrongly. There is nobody behind God forcing Him to fulfill His promises. God Himself must choose to do so. As I suggested earlier, you see the possibility for choosing wrongly in the Garden of Gethsemane. If there was no possibility that Jesus would fail to fulfill His promise, then He would not have sweat blood. He would not have prayed, *Please, if it can be any other way, let it be.* You see the same possibility a few years earlier in Jesus' life, when He is tempted by the devil while in the desert. The temptation would have been completely meaningless if there was no possibility for Jesus to have fallen for it. Thankfully, that God has never broken His promises and even died in order to keep them is clear assurance that He will always be faithful.

So, the origin of the possibility of evil is in God, but there is no evil in God. The creatures that God made in His image also have this possibility, and their choices have often resulted in tragedy. The best known example is the devil. He was, at one time, the most beautiful of all angels but chose to turn away from God. Did you ever notice that the devil is just one person, whereas God is three? The devil is *one* because he is exclusively self-centered. It is his absolute self-centeredness that makes him absolutely evil.

According to Genesis, the devil came to Eve in the Garden and said, *Did God say you couldn't eat anything?* Eve replied, *Oh no, we can eat anything we want, we just can't eat of that tree.* And the devil said, *If you eat of that tree, you will become like God, because God knows good and evil and you will also know good and evil. You won't have to bother God about telling you about good and evil, you'll know for yourself. You can be independent. You can be a liberated woman.* That was appealing to Eve. She was intelligent, she had an adventurous spirit. She took another look at the tree and saw that the fruit was very attractive, and she knew that she really would have the knowledge of good and evil if she ate it, and would be self-sufficient. She wouldn't need God to tell her.

After eating it, Eve gave some to Adam, and then he ate it. At that moment they both died. I don't mean they had heart attacks and fell over. I mean their relationship and their identity died. They knew that they were naked. They knew they were a threat to each other. There was no longer trust. They didn't trust God and they couldn't trust each other. When their relationship died, they were dead. Their true identity had not been in themselves but in their relationship.

Adam and Eve realized there was a problem, and sometimes I think they could have held hands and gone to God and said, 'Father, we have a problem, can you help us?' But they didn't do that because they had become insane. Their thinking was now fundamentally distorted and unhealthy. Instead of going to the Creator for a solution, they reached into creation. They found fig leaves and sewed them together to hide their sexuality, probably because that was what they now found most disturbing and threatening. In reaching into the creation for a solution, we also see the birth of *naturalism*, a belief that we should turn to the physical world in order to solve our problems.

God came into the Garden and called for Adam. Why did He want to talk to Adam if Eve was the one who took the first bite? Here you see the function of hierarchy. Adam was with Eve when she did it, and he was responsible for her. For this reason, God wants to know from Adam what has happened. That's not politically correct, but that's the way God does it.

In confronting Adam, God asks a wonderful question: *Where are you?* Remember that God knows everything. The question is not for God to get information. The question is for Adam, so that he can ask himself where he is. Adam gives a good answer when he replies, *I'm in fear, and nakedness, and hiding.* That was all true. That was his situation.

Then God asks a second question: *Who told you that you were naked?* In other words 'What are your sources and why have you believed them?' He also asks: *Have you eaten of the fruit that I told you not to eat? Did you bring this fear and nakedness and hiding on yourself?* Adam's answer, in this case, could not be worse. He says, *The woman, who you gave to me, offered me the fruit. It's your fault and her fault.* In other words 'I am a victim.' It was here that victimization and denial began. 'I'm not responsible, I'm a victim. I don't need to be forgiven, I'm entitled. I don't need to confess and repent.' This attitude has remained popular in the human race.

God made coats from the skins of animals and clothed them. He killed the innocent and He covered Adam and Eve with the blood of the innocent. It was a visual and applied prophecy of the Crucifixion. Here, and in many other episodes described in the Bible, you can also see how the God of the third circle is not a passive and silent God. He is not a New Age elephant. He is active and communicative. From the beginning, He is deeply engaged with His creation and working faithfully toward its salvation.

Salvation is necessary because ever since the unfaithfulness of Adam and Eve we have been living in a condition of self-centeredness. The human condition has imploded like a supernova—like a huge star that has exploded outward and then reversed direction and collapsed into a black hole, whose gravity is so strong that not even light can escape from it. Everything gets sucked into it. Self-centeredness is what it means to be dead. It's what it means to be a sinner. It's a disastrous situation, and, according to the third circle, it's the cause of suffering in the world.

The Solution

So how do we get out of this mess? The solution is that the Creator Himself enters into the creation and becomes one of us, a human being, made of flesh and blood. Hence the birth of Jesus: *Merry Christmas!* Then, being in the creation and being the Creator, in time and in eternity, natural and supernatural, human and God, immanent and transcendent, He does one thing: He empties Himself. Literally. He sacrifices His life, allowing His body to be nailed to a wooden cross, so that His blood can be drained for others. Jesus gave Himself, emptied Himself, not for Himself but for others. It was, and remains, the ultimate, most astonishing other-centered act in all of history.

The crucifixion of Jesus wasn't just an idea. It wasn't a symbolic gesture. It was an actual, physical emptying for others. Jesus saved us with His blood. We are broken, and God came into the creation and emptied Himself. The power of that emptying, which is dying to self, kills death. Death was killed on the cross. The death that Jesus died was not caused by sin. It was not caused by self-centeredness. The death that Jesus died was caused by perfect love, and so the death was perfect and swallowed up all of death in victory.

This behavior is typical God-behavior. It's the basic nature of God. God is love, and love, according to the first letter of John, is an atoning sacrifice. Atonement means *making it possible to be together*. The meaning is easily remembered if we break the word down into three parts: at–one–ment. Our sin, or self-centeredness, separates us from God, each other and the rest of creation, and Jesus came to make atonement so that we could be together. Jesus shows us what it means to be in the image of God.

Notice that Jesus didn't die on earth and He didn't die in heaven. He was hanging on a cross, suspended in the middle: He bridges heaven and earth. The Roman emperor in those days was called *pontifex maximus*, the Great Bridge Builder, but the title is more fitting for the crucified Christ who connects the Creator and the creation, eternity and time, the immanent and the transcendent, bringing all things together by the power of His word, by the power of His blood, making a new reality. Reality has been divided by sin, and His body is the bridge that crosses the divide. This is Jesus Christ. This is the God-man.

The result of Jesus' death was three days in the tomb, earthquake, darkness, and then resurrection. Resurrection was not resuscitation of a dead body into life. The resurrected body of Christ was raised not like Lazarus who was raised to die again, but to eternal life, into a glorified existence.

The Bible tells us that people who receive the power of Jesus' blood will also become new people. God is a choice-making God, and we as His image are a choice-making people, and so we must choose to receive the power to be remade. It isn't a change of mind. It isn't joining a club. It's a radical turn of being. When we choose to receive the power of the blood of Jesus we are remade. We have been dead self-centered creatures who become living other-centered creatures. The expression the Bible uses to describe this change is *born again*. When we are born as babies, we cannot become unborn, and we eventually die. When we are born again by the blood of Christ, we cannot become unborn, and we do not die. We become new creatures that belong in a new heaven and new earth. We are remade in the power of the Crucifixion. We are no longer self-centered, imploding, dead individuals, but we are re-created as other-centered living people.

Once we have been born again, the rest of our lives is a process of adjusting to becoming other-centered. We grow in love. Our life gets bigger and richer. That is the picture the Bible gives us. It isn't the picture that we see very much in our world. We don't see it much in ourselves; we don't see it much in the church, but it's the picture of God's deepest desire for us. It's a real power that is available to us in Jesus, at this very moment—to become new creatures, turned inside out, reborn, emptying ourselves, losing our lives in order to find them.

That is the Christian solution to suffering.

○　○　○

To Put it Simply

We have explored three circles, or three absolute worldviews, each of which provides a unique hope to the problem of suffering. In the first circle, the original perfection is a total perfect unity and we suffer because we have the illusion of diversity. Salvation is waking up and realizing that unity again. In the second circle, the original perfection is the perfect harmony of equal opposites. We suffer because disharmony or imbalance has come into reality. Salvation is restoring that harmony and balance through various methods and therapies. In the third circle, the original perfection is a unity of three persons who are other-centered in a relational reality of love. We suffer because we have turned things around and have become self-centered dead people. Salvation is God coming into creation and giving Himself in order that people can receive the power to be re-created as other-centered living people.

What do you think? Where are you?

45 QUESTIONS

Asking honest questions is a sign of life. During the many years I have lectured and spoken with people about the three circles, hundreds of questions have been raised. Such questions are invaluable as they connect people more directly and practically with my teaching and keep us away from mechanical on–off, black–white responses. We grow and learn by asking.

My hope is that the following questions, translated from various languages, may stimulate your thoughts and provoke further topics for discussion among you.

o o o

Do you truly believe it's possible to simplify so vast and complex a subject as the cosmos into one of your theoretical circles?

No, it's not. The three circles are grossly reductionistic symbol sets. I hope they will be useful, but they are not adequate. Objective truth in the form of a symbol is not sufficient to express the Truth. Truth is also subjective, which means that explanations involving symbols must be combined with your personal subjective experience to produce reality. You cannot merely think about Jesus and be a Christian any more than you can think about matrimony and have a marriage. The reality of being married is much larger than any kind of symbol. Still, symbols can be helpful.

What is the Monist's view of spiritual evolution?

In most cases people in the first circle see the human being as a high level of consciousness, evolved from a life force that manifests itself in increasingly complex ways and increasingly self-aware ways. Animals, such as flies or worms or rats, would not have individual consciousness. The human being has individual consciousness and makes choices as an individual. The human is also reincarnated in the same consciousness, albeit without an awareness of the past, whereas the consciousness of the rat or fly would dissolve into unconsciousness when it dies. Although other life-forms suffer, they don't have the possibility to realize unity and stop suffering until they evolve and focus in human individual consciousness. To be a human being in terms of the whole of reality is considered very precious. The human being has the possibility of enlightenment. The belief that humans live and die thousands of times might also make people of the first circle more patient. If you don't manage something in this life, don't panic, because there is another life. This view can make you more relaxed and reduce stress, which in many ways can be healthy. Still, we need to consider things within the whole context of what is real and to ask, 'Do we pay too big a price for the therapy that we experience?'

How do people of monistic religions see marriage?

In the first circle, marriage is something that people do as a helpful exercise in the early stages of development, because marriage is a form of uniting and becoming one. But when you are very advanced in your incarnations, you go and live in a monastery. There are very religious people in India who get married and raise children and have a business, but when their children leave home they sometimes sell the business and separate, and one goes to a monastery and the other goes to a nunnery. They release each other for advancement, because they realize that they have become a handicap to each other. They have experienced a union in the marriage, but it's also an attachment. They have to separate in order to increase in Buddha-nature or Krishna consciousness.

How do people of monistic religions explain increases or changes in the human population?

The appearance of more human beings on the earth reflects the movement of more groups of life-forms into human individual consciousness. Those individual consciousnesses are manifest in the birth of babies. A new baby may be someone who is born for the thousandth time or for the first time. The baby could be much older than the parents in terms of evolutionary progression. That might be an explanation for the genius of Mozart; he may have been an older person with lots of experience behind him. The population of humans can get larger or smaller according to the wisdom of the Lords of Karma. Human beings function under the decisions of the Lords of Karma, which deals with so many variables that we cannot comprehend them.

You suggested that there is no genuine right and wrong in Monism. Doesn't the idea of karma, however, implicitly recognize the concepts of right and wrong, and therefore a general moral structure?

Karma operates within the illusion of maya, of diversity, of particularity and relationships. In that illusion there are positive and negative situations, energies, and vibrations that are established and created and which need to be brought into harmony in order for Buddha-nature or Krishna consciousness to be realized. Karma is an extremely rich and complicated process. The long-range goal is to become liberated in Buddha-nature or Krishna consciousness. The working out of karma, however, can occur in a variety of ways. Consider the example of murder. If I murder somebody in this lifetime, then in my next lifetime I might be murdered, or I might save lives. Either possibility could produce a balance in my karma, even though the two possibilities are very different. One is passive and results in death, the other is active and results in life. Karma is not a retributive judicial system. It has that element in it, but there are other major elements intertwined with it, so you can't understand karma purely in moral terms. It's larger and broader and richer than that.

You mentioned that in the monistic worldview relationships are evil, and love is also evil, because love is a relationship. If this is the case, then why does Buddhism emphasize compassion so strongly?

Your question equates compassion with love, which is a mistake. Love involves relationship, but compassion is a realization of unity and identity. When I have compassion for someone, I support their movement toward the realization of Buddha-nature or Krishna consciousness in the context of many, many reincarnated lifetimes. Let me give you an example. If a person is born into a life of suffering, it's possible they may be working out their karma based on the wisdom of the Lords of Karma about what is most profitable for that person. For this reason, if I see that person suffering, I should avoid helping him because I understand that he might have to suffer all over again if I interfere in his process. This reasoning is the basis for the Buddhist doctrine of non-interference. It may seem cruel not to help a suffering person, but in the context of reincarnation it might be the most compassionate thing to do, because by not interfering with the person's suffering you are allowing that person to bring their karma into balance. The Christian idea of love is very different, because the context in which it occurs is very different. There is only one lifetime in which all significance of our being and choice-making is concentrated. There is also a fundamental belief in the eternal reality of relationships. The love of Christ is a love of relationships, of seeing face-to-face, of encouraging each other to be ourselves as God made us to be. Poverty and suffering are seen as distortions of God's intention for human life and are things to be worked against. Christians have a mandate to relieve the suffering of others and to respect everybody's individual life. So compassion and love are not synonymous, although we hear them used that way in the culture at large. The Bible has the word compassion, but it's very closely connected to love.

Buddhism recognizes that depression and other forms of emotional suffering are connected to narcissism, egotism, and an obsession with the self, and it provides methods to treat this suffering. In what ways does Christianity add to our understanding of emotional suffering and healing?

The idea that depression and emotional suffering are a result of narcissism and egotism is, in many cases, quite accurate. The same basic idea can be found in the Bible. The Buddhist and Christian perspectives differ, however, with respect to the context of the suffering and the cure. For Buddhists, the choice is between self and SELF, between individual egocentric self and universal Buddha-nature SELF. The Christian choice is between self-centered and other-centered. As a result, the Buddhist solution to suffering has the goal of dissolving the self into the absolute SELF. The Christian solution has the goal of reorienting the self in the direction of *others*—toward other people and toward God. The individual self is preserved, not dissolved, and heals and develops through a relationship of love with the rest of reality. That is the basic meaning of salvation through Jesus Christ. Christianity values the need to heal depression, and it values healing practices in general (whether Buddhist or otherwise), but it would not sacrifice the unique reality of the person, of God, or the reality of love, in exchange for healing or freedom from suffering.

New Age people emphasize the power of belief. What do you think of that?

The idea, if I understand it, is that we create reality through our thinking. If we think negatively we create a more negative reality, and if we think positively we produce a more positive reality. Positive thinking in biblical terms always occurs in the context of Jesus. It's not really about *us* creating reality but trusting that God will create *for* us the reality that we need in order to carry out His purpose for our lives. What He creates might please us, or it might be at odds with what we want. Either way, we should be grateful and trusting and work with what God gives us.

If children color mandalas in school, will they be drawn to Hinduism?

Maybe, but they will be no more drawn to Hinduism by coloring mandalas than to Jesus by coloring crosses.

Is meditation dangerous for Christians?

It would be different for different people. For some people, it could be therapeutic. For some psychological conditions it could be very dangerous. It's also very dangerous if we think that meditating will forgive our sins, or that it will give us our true identity, or if we meditate instead of praying.

Is there a Christian practice of meditation?

The phrase 'Christian practice of meditation' is associated with a whole history and practice of ideas that is too large to address here. Allow me to narrow the question to a more specific consideration of the *biblical* practice of meditation. While Eastern meditation seeks to stop the mind or hold it still, biblical meditation starts with some content about God, holds it over the mind as over a web or net, and allows the Holy Spirit to touch the mind with it. Then the person thinks and prays about the connection they have experienced. Biblical meditation is not directional and does not have an agenda. It's more passive and receptive than thinking, but it is connected to thinking.

Atheism is a major worldview today.
Where does it fit among your three circles?

Atheism is the belief that there is no God and that all things emerge by chance from the material substance of the universe. Many atheists believe that the universe began with a singularity, or a unity of all energy in a single point that exploded outward in an event called the *big bang*. After the big bang, diversity is believed to have entered the universe through the emergence of various physical laws and physical phenomena including stars, planets, and eventually the earth with its various characteristics, including biological life as we know it. None of these physical facts, however, can have absolute meaning in atheism. Atheists can experience a *feeling* of meaning, in the sense of feeling as if their life is meaningful, or as if their relationships are meaningful, or as if sunsets and mountain ranges are meaningful, but if there is no actual absolute meaning in the universe—if the universe is an impersonal and accidental thing—then anything that occurs within the universe cannot be absolutely meaningful either, no matter how much we may feel or believe it to be. In an atheistic universe, meaning is essentially an illusion. Although atheists may not regard themselves as Monists, you can see the similarity in their viewpoints: the universe begins in a state of unity, and then gives rise to a diversity that is actually an illusion. People of the third circle, on the other hand, assume that the universe and everything in it is absolutely meaningful because it was created by a God who is intrinsically meaningful. Life, as a result, is not fundamentally an illusion. It seems to me to take a great deal more faith to be an atheist than to be a Christian, because you have to maintain the idea that a blind, meaningless, purposeless, amoral, uncaring, directionless reality has produced human beings who are the opposite of all these characteristics. A simpler assumption is that the characteristics of humanness are an expression of something inherent within the universe itself, and something that pre-exists the universe. To paraphrase the Bible: *in the beginning there was Information.*

I think the attraction of atheism for many people is that it relieves them of the burden of having to think deeply about *why* they exist. It also relieves them of any idea of guilt or sin. If there is no absolute meaning, there can be no real justification for feelings of guilt or a belief in right and wrong. Again, the lack of any absolute meaning in categories like right and wrong makes atheism quite similar to Monism. Some atheists also believe that after expanding for a period of time, the universe will collapse again into singularity, or total unity, which is not unlike the Monist's view. Other atheists, however, believe the universe will expand endlessly. Given the many similarities between Monism and atheism, I would say that atheism can be regarded as part of the first circle or a variation of the first circle.

Christians sometimes adopt a defensive posture to the good they see in non-Christians. An example would be a statement like: Well, it was nice of those atheists to contribute to a good cause, but—and the but may be followed by—they don't have Jesus, or they are going to hell in the end, or some other statement that has the effect of discounting the goodness of another human being. Have you witnessed this attitude toward non-Christian acts of goodness, and what thoughts do you have about it?

I have seen that attitude, but less recently than in previous years I'm glad to say. I think it's out of place in the kingdom of God not to recognize goodness when we see it, and not to believe that all human beings have eternity in their hearts. In a fundamental sense, it's not possible to please God without faith, but I think it's possible to express His image in a variety of ways, in some cases more accurately by the non-Christian than by the Christian. But those expressions of goodness, if they're not contextualized and completed by Jesus Christ, are not integrated. They are not held together. They are bits and snatches and incomplete. The goodness of the Christian, even if in some cases less than that of the non-Christian, is completed in Christ. In the idea of the writer of Hebrews, *all things are held together in Christ by the word of His power.* Either way, there is no room for sneering about another person's act of goodness. There is room for admiration and praise and self-rebuke.

Have you benefited from your contact with atheists?

Yes. I think I've learned something about what it means to be human and made in the image of God from atheists—in particular from those who practice patience and discipline in ways that I don't, and from those who practice creativity, courage, and the embrace of life in ways better than I have. So I have learned from some atheists about what it means to be a human being. I don't learn from them what it means to have my sins forgiven or to be completed in Christ, but I have learned lots of other things.

Into which of the three circles do animistic and shamanistic worldviews fit? Where would Judaism and Islam fit?

Remember that the circles are a reductionistic and approximated system. They address the fundamental aspects of different worldviews rather than surface details. Bearing this in mind, I suggest that animism and shamanism would fit into the first or second circle, or some combination of the two, depending on individual understanding or practices. Judaism as we find it in the Old Testament, or Torah, would fit the third circle. In the creation account, God speaks among Himself, and later He appeared to Abraham as three men. You have the whole Trinity in the Old Testament. In the understanding and practice and thought of Jews, however, you will see some leaning toward the first circle. In the

Koran, you have fundamentally the first circle. Allah is one. There is no other. He has no son. There is a very strong unity and absoluteness in Allah. He is not intrinsically relational. If Allah wants to talk to somebody and function as a personal god, then he has to create somebody to talk to.

Some people might wonder why bother with worldviews? Why not just live life as best you can? What are your thoughts about that?

You can to a large extent try to live like that, without any particular direction or context. You couldn't hold any strong ideas, or have any committed purpose, because you wouldn't believe that anything was right or wrong, fitting or unfitting, and probably you would slip into the idea that 'what is right is what feels good, and what is wrong is what feels bad, and I am the judge. I am God.' At the same time, living life 'as best you can' implies a worldview of some kind, even if it's not clearly defined. That's a key issue. We all need a worldview to have a frame and foundation for any meaning and purpose in life, and to provide a justification for our actions. To put it another way, choosing to live as best you can requires some way to measure *best,* and the context of measuring *best* is a worldview. We can bother with the worldview or not, acknowledge it or not, but it's always there.

Do you think the simpler life is happier and more joyful?

Not necessarily. Riches and money and property and knowledge can add burdens to our lives, and give us greater responsibility and more choices, but I don't think they automatically make us more happy or less happy. Many wealthy people and many intelligent people are not happy at all, and many simple people are also bitter and unhappy. I think more important than happiness are values like truth, faithfulness, and godliness. Jesus was full of joy, but He was a man of sorrows as well. The apostle Paul was full of joy, riches, life, assurance, and thankfulness, but he was burdened with many troubles. People betrayed him, he was beaten up, he was thrown in prison. Happiness was not the highest value for Paul or Jesus. I believe that the way God has made us to be, and working toward that way—embracing and confronting the struggles of a fallen world—lead to the best and fullest life but maybe not the happiest life. That's hard to accept because we want to be happy, yet happiness is only a part of reality. It's not wise to sacrifice the other parts of reality in order to be happy. Sometimes I am happy and I enjoy it very much, but happiness is not the main thing.

Do you regard Christianity as a religion?

Religion is a system of connecting with the supernatural. Christianity, as I understand it, is not primarily a system and not primarily about the supernatural. It's the reality of all things both natural and supernatural being held together by Jesus, and our living out that reality. The Pharisees in the time of Jesus were very religious—with their ceremonies, rules, special clothes, and schedules—but Jesus was unimpressed with them. He said that people's righteousness had to be greater than the Pharisees', which means the righteousness of Christians cannot be a set of regulations or a tradition or something ceremonial. It has to be a righteousness of the heart. It's a radical and personal transformation of the heart. There is nothing religious about that.

Many Christians focus excessively on going to heaven. What are your thoughts about that?

Understood correctly, what the Bible teaches is that we must work and pray so that the kingdom of God will become realized on earth. Jesus said, *Pray like this: Our Father in heaven, may Your name be known as holy, Your kingdom come, Your will be done, on earth as it is in heaven.* We recite that prayer but often we don't mean it. Sometimes what we really mean is 'my Father in heaven, please get me out of here!' That's what we have in our hearts. But that isn't what Jesus taught. He taught us to pray, and to work, that the kingdom of heaven will be on earth—that the biblical values and description of human life and relationships will be realized on earth. We're not supposed to just wait and endure it until God jerks us out of here to some other place. But I am sympathetic to the reasons why people have that attitude. We suffer, we are oppressed, we are frustrated. Still, the attitude is wrong, and we need to repent. It's partly because Christians have these wrong ideas that Christianity looks bad to non-Christians—and then we wonder why our evangelism is not very effective. Evangelism will never be effective when we preach a gospel of withdrawal and escapism.

A lot of your ideas, such as objectivity and subjectivity, dynamism, and form and freedom, are not explicitly mentioned in the Bible. Have you encountered theologians who have argued that these ideas are too abstract or speculative to be justified by the actual biblical text?

Very rarely do people make a statement that the ideas I am teaching are not biblical. More often people ask how I discern these ideas in the Bible, which is encouraging. Then I try to work with the question. An example of such a question would be, 'Why do you use the word Trinity, if it's not in the Bible?' In my understanding, the term *Trinity* is a verbal symbol for God's nature as described in the Bible. Another example of a verbal symbol is the Creeds of the Church Fathers. We call them *creeds* because they start with *credo*, or 'I believe', but the Church Fathers called them symbols and definitions because they were a representation of the whole truth in the Bible. In general, you will not find total correspondence between a symbol and the thing being symbolized. Similarly, you will not find total correspondence between verbal symbols, such as the Trinity, form and freedom, or dynamism, and the vocabulary of the Bible, even though such symbols are substantiated by the text of the Bible.

Can you say more about what it's like to be saved, and what happens afterward?

Being saved is like being remade from a dead, self-centered creature into a living, other-centered creature. To be saved is to turn from our brokenness and to begin to move in the direction of healing. That means receiving healing *and* working for healing, or as the old song goes, *trust and obey*. It's a complementarity, a 200% reality. We aren't saved by trusting God *or* obeying him, but by both. Some people get caught, thinking it's one or the other. The question *Which do you choose?* comes, I believe, directly from the devil. *Do you trust in God's healing, or work toward healing?* That's an evil question. It's like asking Humpty Dumpty which side of the wall he wants to fall on. But God says we can have both sides. Jesus says, *I have come that you might have life and have it abundantly. I am not telling you to pick the part of life you want to have. Have the whole thing. Live the whole thing.* To give another example of how we can be challenged after we're saved, consider Psalm 23. This psalm tells us, *My cup runs over.* In reality, when life *runs over* people usually react by thinking 'Oh, what a mess, let's clean this up!' People don't want things to be out of control or unpredictable. But a lack of control is unacceptable only when we walk by sight. When we walk by faith, it's acceptable because we trust in God to stabilize us in the overflowing and abundance of life. Faith can be so frightening because we are not seeing, we are not controlling, we are not totally understanding. We are walking and trusting God. It's as if you hear His voice at the end of a dark tunnel and walk toward His voice. People want to touch the walls. They want to run back and forth. They want to orient themselves. That's natural. Walking by faith is spiritual. We are drawn to the natural because we're fallen and broken. We need to turn and become spiritual. That doesn't mean to abandon the natural, but to contextualize the natural in the fullness of God's truth and reality. Some people think you've got the natural on one side and the spiritual on the other, so that you have to leave one side and come to the other when you're saved. But the biblical picture is that the natural is contextualized within the spiritual, within the Lordship of Jesus Christ. Then nothing is lost. Everything is gained. Life gets bigger and fuller.

If life gets bigger after being saved, why do we often get the opposite impression—that Christian life makes people more limited and rigid?

A question I often ask people in different countries is, 'If you went into your city and stopped ten people, and said, "I would like to ask you a question. If you would become a Christian today, do you think your life would become larger, fuller, and more engaged, or smaller, narrower, and less engaged?"—if you asked that, how would the people answer?' Generally, everyone says that the people would answer the latter; they would think that life becomes smaller, narrower, and less engaged. And I agree that that would be most people's impression. But then I ask, 'Is that what the Bible says?' They say, 'No, that isn't what the Bible says.' I agree with that, too. So where do people get the idea that becoming a Christian makes you more limited? They get it to some extent from the media and from false attacks against Christianity, but to a large degree they get it from Christians themselves. If that is the truth, then maybe the beginnings of apologetics should be an apology. Maybe we should ask people whether they can forgive us for giving them the wrong idea about what it means to live as a Christian. We also need to practice the Lordship of Jesus Christ over *all* of life, not just the religious life.

A key image of Christianity is the Crucifixion and the washing away of our sins with the blood of Christ. The image is violent, and for many people disturbing and hard to relate to. Is there any other way to convey the central message of Christianity?

Blood is it. Death is it. It can never be nice. I sometimes tell people it's like going to the dentist. A saving visit to the dentist can never be nice—not if you have a good dentist. Suppose you have a terrible toothache and the dentist says, 'Oh, you must be in awful pain. Here, let me bless you. Have some morphine.' If he then walks away and that's his solution, he hasn't blessed you, he's cursed you. To bless you is initially to *increase* the pain. The dentist is a clear example of the painful blessing. Sometimes it can be helpful to remind people that life is not nice, and to have *more life* is not a totally nice process. Of course, people naturally prefer to imagine a nice kind of salvation. You can imagine a Buddhist or transcendental kind of thing—and a lot of people do. It's very natural and romantic to imagine a nice salvation. But the Bible doesn't give a nice salvation. It's a scandal. Paul himself says this. It's always been true. Jesus is falsely advertised as totally nice, but He isn't. He's real.

C. S. Lewis got it right in *The Lion, the Witch and the Wardrobe*. The children in the story are wondering about Aslan, a kind of symbol for Jesus, and ask, *Is he safe?* And they are told, *Of course he isn't safe. But he's good.* Safe or nice doesn't mean good. Another illustration would be a mother with her three-year-old boy about to cross the street. If the boy tries to run into a street where the cars are going back and forth, the mother's love would be expressed very violently. She would grab that little boy and jerk him off the street at risk of breaking his arm. She might shout and try to instill fear in him. And that will be her love. If, on the other hand, she had been nice, then he would have died. Our situation is urgent, and God's solution is drastic and effective.

Is God a male according to the Bible, or does He include anything of the female?

God is absolute, and from God proceed both male and female. In the Bible, we are taught to call God *Father*, but we can see in various places that He is also Mother. In the Old Testament, God says: *I would comfort you as one's own mother comforts him.* In the New Testament, Jesus says to Jerusalem that He would gather it as a mother hen gathers her chicks. We customarily call God Father in part because of His relationship with Jesus. Also, some prominent characteristics of God expressed through history demonstrate that He is powerful and law-giving—this leans in the direction of fatherhood. Still, although it would be accurate to pray to God the Father, to regard God *as a whole* as only Father would not be accurate, because God is larger than that.

What is the difference between angels and fallen angels based on your understanding?

God is three persons and other-centered. The devil is one person and self-centered. For this reason, the angels who follow God are other-centered, and the angels who follow the devil are self-centered. They are like black holes, sucking things into them. That is why the devil and fallen angels relate to people by possessing and consuming them. The angels of God, on the other hand, bless people, encourage people to be other-centered, to love, and to know the Truth.

Have Christians misread the Bible in ways that result in the misuse or exploitation of nature?

Yes. An example would be escapism eschatology. This is the belief that at the end of the world Jesus is going to come and take us away to someplace else, and burn His creation and start over in some heavenly realm. I don't believe this idea is supported by the Bible, but it has been believed by Christians and has resulted in a utilitarian attitude of 'use creation for your own purposes, because God hates it and is going to burn it up anyway.' This attitude is one of the main criticisms that New Age people and Buddhists have against Christians, and the criticism is valid.

Some would suggest the Bible is easy to misuse and misunderstand because of its complexity. Why would God create such a complex document to express His truth? Why not create something simpler?

God is complex and His image is complex. A simple expression of truth would be reductive, inadequate, and inappropriate. There is a limit on the simplicity that there can be in God's relationship to us. If it's too simple, then people will be puppets and automatons. There must be room to think and choose. God is not automatic and so His image cannot be automatic. The Bible is not unlike other things in life—marriage, for instance. Marriage is complex, and hard to understand and prone to misuse, but that doesn't mean we should get rid of it or avoid it. The fact that the Bible is complex and people misuse it deliberately or accidentally doesn't show me that the Bible is wrong. It shows me that it's realistic.

Is salvation possible for people of non-Christian religions, or for people who don't practice any religion?

Yes, not because everything is true, but because God puts eternity in the hearts of all people. We are promised that if we seek Him with all our heart, we will find Him. The reverse is also true. Many people who identify themselves as Christians are far from Christianity. You can go to a lot of churches and find people who are not Christian. You will find jealousy, pride, manipulation, greed, ecologically unsound ideas, and all sorts of problems. We are called by Jesus to be His ambassadors, and to demonstrate His reality in our relationships with each other, but we fail. That failure doesn't mean that no one can be saved. I know a lot of missionaries, and I've heard amazing stories about how people are saved without meeting a Christian. So, yes, I think that people who are without the Bible or a church, if they are honest, can know their need of God. They can become poor in spirit—the kind of people Jesus called *blessed*. If they are honest, they will cry out to God and God will answer. That's a personal, individual issue, not a religious or racial or cultural issue.

Are you saying that people can be saved without Jesus?

No, I don't mean they can be saved without Jesus, but they can be saved outside of the cultural tradition of the church. God can come to them directly. I have met people who became Christians because of a vision. I knew a missionary woman who went to Indonesia and entered a remote valley with translators. The people had never met a foreigner, and she told them, 'I have come to tell you about the Lamb of God who came to take away the sins of the world.' They said, 'We know that.' She said, 'Who told you?'

The people then recounted the story of a man, now deceased, who had been the judge of that particular tribe. The man had apparently lived in anguish for a long time because, although he was the judge of others, there was nobody to judge *him*. He couldn't live with that. He cried out, and one day he saw a vision of a lamb being slain. It was a vision of Saint John in the Apocalypse, and he understood that the Creator had died to make him just and right, and then he believed. He had never heard the word *Jesus*, but he believed in Jesus, and he taught his people to the extent of his understanding. It happens like that sometimes. That doesn't mean we don't have to tell people. We are responsible to do what we can do. But we don't need to live in despair and to think that God is cruel and unfair because of the people we cannot meet.

How can Christians connect more closely with people of the first and second circles?

That's a good question, because most people in the world are Monists or Dualists of one kind or another. If you are a Christian, there is a good chance you will have a Monist or Dualist as a neighbor. Christians know that they need to love their neighbor. To love somebody you need to understand them, because love is not a feeling. Love is a relationship with other people involving understanding, communicating, and supporting. And love is not debating and arguing. If I know everything and I win all the debates but there is no love, then it's garbage. We need to understand people in order to love them, and only then can the logic and the discussion be really valuable. It also helps to remember what Christians and non-Christians have in common. God made me a Christian, but before that He made me a human being. When I became a Christian, I did not cease to be a human being. As a Christian, there are many things I don't have in common with other people, whereas on the level of being human, there are many things I do have in common with other people. The other thing I would add is the importance of listening to people and asking deeply human questions. What does it mean to be a human being? How do we know ourselves? What is my meaning or purpose? How can I deal with my guilt? Where did everything come from and where is it going? These are the questions that everybody struggles with. Those of us who are Christians know the answer is Jesus, but *what are the questions?* That's where we need to work with people and bless people. We mustn't say to people 'I don't care what your questions are, believe in Jesus, He's the answer.' That's not love, that's just selling something. We need to ask 'What are your questions?' Then we can hopefully say 'Yes, those are my questions too! We are human. We live in a difficult world.' Then we can start exploring the answers.

You emphasize the importance of asking questions. Where in the Bible are we encouraged to ask questions or show curiosity?

God invites us to reason with Him. You see it in various places. In Isaiah 1:18 God says: *Come let us reason together.* In Genesis, God evangelizes Adam with a series of questions: *Where are you? Who told you? Have you eaten?* If this is God's evangelistic methodology, we would be wise to follow it by asking questions of each other. Also, I think asking questions is one of the reasons why Jesus wants us to be like little children. How many of you have ever known a little child that did not ask questions? Those kinds of children don't exist. It's their job to ask questions. God doesn't want us to stop thinking. He wants us to ask, to test everything—touch it, feel it, squeeze it.

Non-Christians often attend your talks. What kinds of perspectives do they bring?

I find that non-Christians often bring a fresher perspective than Christians. I think it's because non-Christians are not coming from the same cultural, traditional religious grid. Their questions are not expressed in religious jargon. They're more often expressed in common English, German, Russian, or what have you. When a Christian asks a question, they expect it to be answered within the context of the Christian worldview and traditional cultural experience, which is not the whole human reality. The Christians' questions that I get are rather predictable. Non-Christians tend to be less predictable. That gets your adrenaline going and keeps you awake. I enjoy it.

What are the unique challenges for Christians when it comes to asking questions?

I think a difficulty with born-again Christians is that they know that they are born again into the peace of God, but they think that this peace means a lack of conflict. But that isn't what the Bible means when it says *peace*. It means *shalom*, which is a foundation of well-being and understanding of reality. It's the foundation on which to have conflicts and to ask questions, and to confess to not knowing and needing to know more. Many Christians are passive and complacent in their faith, forgetting that the word *Israel* means *the one who wrestles with God*.

Doesn't asking questions provoke a sense of uncertainty and doubt, which can have the effect of weakening faith?

Asking questions makes it easier to hold on to faith in the things that the Bible wants us to believe in. If we never question in doubt, then we will never grow in understanding. The Bible wants us to believe in a personal God and a personal relationship with that God. The Bible wants us to receive people's questions, and to ask our own questions about reality. Not asking questions means our faith is weak. It means we don't trust God to sustain us in the process of crisis and confusion. There is no growth without asking questions. In verses five and seven of the fourth chapter of Proverbs, we are commanded to *get wisdom*. This means that we don't already have it. One of the ways to start getting it is by asking questions.

How does your current church community react to your questions?

Slowly but positively. Many of the questions I find in the Bible and bring to the Bible are paradigm-shifting questions. It takes most people a long time to come to grips with this kind of questioning, and it requires a lot of gentle repetition.

How can we learn to ask better questions?

There are a variety of ways. Read books that ask questions. Read novels and see films that ask questions, and think about the biblical answers. Realize that some answers aren't tied up with a bow. Think things through down to the bottom and out to the edges. Be courageous and rigorous in asking dangerous questions. Don't shy away from frightening questions. Ask questions for which you don't already have a supposed answer. Think about why the question is being asked. What difference will the answer make to your life? If your questions come out verbally garbled, try writing them down. The process is endless. You have to stay awake.

Why did you originally become a Buddhist?

I grew up in a Christian atmosphere and I kept asking absolute questions. But the Christians I knew were not interested in my questions. They said, 'Don't ask questions, just believe. Become like a little child and have faith without asking questions.' That didn't make sense to me. It was only later when I came to realize that, in telling us to become like little children, Jesus really did want us to ask and inquire and explore. As a result of my early dissatisfaction with Christianity, I began shopping around and tried out different philosophies and religions. I was in the Rosicrucian Society, the Bahai, the Self-Realization Fellowship of Paramahansa Yogananda, and other groups. I settled on Zen Buddhism because it's very unreligious. Zen Buddhists are always interested in absolutes, and I was interested in absolutes. I also appreciated the fact that they were the only religious group I knew that did not sell jewelry.

How did you become a Christian?

There are various true answers. One true answer is by free will. Another true answer is by the sovereign working of the Holy Spirit. A correct answer must include both: I choose and God chooses. In terms of the specifics of my choosing, I can think of several concrete reasons. Among the most important ones was the realization that it takes less faith to believe in Christianity than to believe in anything else. It takes more faith, in my understanding, to believe in humanism. I know people who believe that human beings are fundamentally good, and I think, wow, what faith! They believe against all the evidence! Such a powerful faith! I don't want to have a faith like that. Too much faith is destructive. I want to have a small faith in a big truth. I don't want a big faith in a wrong idea. A human being can believe anything. A human being can believe that the world is flat, and they can believe it strongly enough that they are willing to die or kill for it. But the faith that the world is flat does not make the world flat. My faith that Jesus is God and Lord does not make Him God and Lord. If He is God and Lord, then He is that independent of my believing in Him. That was important to me during my search—a truth that was independent of my faith—and the most independent understanding I found was in the biblical worldview. I also asked a lot of questions as I studied Christianity. There was a thought-loop that ran in my head for weeks. I had once sung in an English opera called *The Mikado,* and one of the lines of the opera was 'who are you who ask this question?' I kept hearing this line in my head while I was studying, and I thought, maybe I should pay attention to this. Then I thought, I am asking all these questions, but who is asking? I realized that the Buddhist answer is *Asking is,* but the Christian answer is *I am asking.* That was closer to my actual experience of myself. I had been asking questions all my life. So that was another reason why Christianity made sense to me. But I didn't struggle with things that most people do. Many people struggle with either guilt and the denial of guilt, or they struggle with the existence of the supernatural. Some are naturalists, like many scientists and engineers, who believe that if you can't measure something and express it in numbers then it doesn't exist. But I never had those difficulties. I was a supernaturalist all my life.

What difficulties did you have?

The thing that was crucial to me was the personal nature of reality. One of my questions was: Is the non-personal necessarily sub-personal? Couldn't there be a super-personal, non-personal, from which personality could proceed? To put it another way, can human reality, which is personal, result from an absolute reality that is impersonal, or can an impersonal absolute reality only result in things that are less than personal? That was a very serious question for me, and it was very difficult to find a Christian who would take it seriously, or who could even begin to understand what the question was. The Buddhist answer to the question is *Yes*—an impersonal absolute realty can give rise to a personal human reality in the illusion of diversity—but the Christian answer is *No*—only a personal absolute reality can create a personal human reality. I wanted to know why Christians believed in their answer, and why the Buddhist answer might not be right. The Lord had to guide me to the L'Abri Fellowship in Switzerland before I could even find people who could understand my questions and help me. But that was my own unique struggle. We are each different. I can tell you how and why I came to be a Christian, but you cannot do it that way. You have to do it your own way. You are not me. You are unique. You have to come to God and God has to come to you in a way that you understand intellectually, emotionally, existentially, and morally, in ways that I might not understand. According to the Bible, your relationship to God is like a marriage. Christians often speak of sharing their faith, but I don't believe I can share my faith. I think I can share *the* faith—what is believed by Christians—but I cannot share *my* faith any more than I can share my marriage. I have a marriage, and I can tell you about it, but I cannot share it with you. I have a faith in Jesus Christ, and I can tell you about it, but I cannot share it with you. You have to have your own. You cannot have it by copying another person, or by inheriting it from your parents or your grandparents. We can say that God has no grandchildren. He only has children. Each one has to come directly to Him.

Given that you're the kind of person who continues to ask questions about worldviews, do you think it's possible that you might one day find a different answer and abandon Christianity?

I want to be careful that my Christianity doesn't become fanaticism, or something that I believe because I believe. If someone proved that they'd found the bones of Jesus, I would cease to be a Christian at that moment, because it wouldn't be true. There are parts about being a Christian that I enjoy, but I would sacrifice those for truth. I think you have to stay open, but at the same time faithful and committed. You might meet a lot of interesting women, but you should only marry one of them. That means you need to say *No* to many women and *Yes* to just one. The relationship with Jesus, as I've already mentioned, is like a marriage. If you would discover that the woman you married has serious problems and was married eight times before and has nine children that you didn't know about, then you might leave that situation. In a similar way, if I discovered that Jesus was a lie, then I would go through a fundamental crisis. And as far as I can imagine now, I would go back to Zen Buddhism. But the falsity of Christianity would have to be really established in various ways for me to give up my faith in it.

Do you still encounter people in the church now who tell you 'don't ask, just believe'?

Much less—partly because I am older and people want to be polite, and partly because I now pastor in a church where many of the people do scientific research. Their entire careers are about asking questions.

I find it interesting, however, that many Christians who are scientists and researchers will separate their scientific work from their religious faith. They will say 'this is faith but that is knowledge.' That's schizophrenic. I don't think it's healthy. It's so common probably because to compartmentalize is to simplify and to have control, and people feel good about doing that. But I'm always encouraging people to put things together. Everything belongs together in Jesus. When you read the Bible, you should not only ask 'Do I believe it?' but also 'What does it mean?' You never finish finding out. You have to stay awake. You have to stay as a little child.

Your attitude of openness and curiosity is unusual for a pastor. Does that reflect your years of practice as a Buddhist?

I don't know. There are certainly some things I have retained from my Zen Buddhist background that are good. They are not things you can't find in the Bible, but they are things that Christians have not emphasized much. The main one is the idea of the importance of the ordinary. In Zen, the ordinary things are special and the special things are ordinary. I think that's biblical, although Christians themselves have tended to ignore the ordinary and value the special things, the special experiences, the special places, the special holy hardware. In Ecclesiastes we are encouraged to dig in the garden and eat and be thankful to God. It's very ordinary. The Zen emphasis on the ordinary also includes valuing creation. Zen Buddhists don't know that God created it, but they value it. One of the great sayings of Zen is: *Buddha is a manure pile.* This means that if you don't recognize Buddha in the manure pile when you're shoveling in the garden, then you don't know Buddha. As a result, Zen Buddhists tend not to exploit or abandon nature. They try to incorporate nature into Buddha-nature. The Bible gives us responsibility to take care of the creation that God loves, but Christians sometimes stray from that.

Do you have a denominational preference?

My own personal practice has Baptist and Brethren tendencies. I can, however, see great value in liturgy. I certainly enjoy it. I see value in the systematic living out of God's salvific history and His word through symbol and text and activity, rather than through a haphazard 'as the occasion arises' or 'as the mood strikes' sort of approach. At the same time, there are dangers that we may begin to worship the tradition of the liturgy itself. Also, many people who are in liturgical churches have very little idea of what any of it means. They do it because it's done. They may practice it for a sense of belonging, or social advantage, or out of habit. Someone once referred to liturgy as *truth hidden by many sacred veils*. I think that may be the case for many people.

Do you experience life's pain as less painful because you are a Christian?

No. It's more hopeful, but I don't experience less pain. There may be *more* pain, in fact. The pain of a Christian is not only their own pain, but the pain of the world, the pain that Christ feels for humanity—not that I am particularly acute in this sensitivity compared to others. Still, I think that in the Christian life, as people walk the walk and run the race, one becomes more sensitive rather than less sensitive. Life becomes more intense, richer, fuller, with more pain and more joy.

What is one of the most important answers you have received from the Bible?

The fourth chapter of Philippians is very precious to me. Paul tells us not to be anxious about anything, but in everything, in all the circumstances and details of your life, by prayer and supplication, bring your requests to God. Don't hide anything from God. Bring everything. Tell Him your point of view. Tell Him what you want. You're not God, you don't see perfectly, but tell Him what you want. Find out how you see things and what you think a good way would be and then tell God. Now, if you do this, the promise is pointedly *not* that God will give you what you ask for. That would be a terrible curse. One of the worst wishes you can have for another person is 'may you get what you want.' They'll surely be destroyed. So God doesn't say He'll give us what we want. The promise is that He will *keep* us. *The peace of God, which passes all understanding, will keep your hearts and minds through Jesus Christ.* That is the promise. What are the details of the outworking of that promise? They are infinite. We don't know what that promise-keeping will look like from one person to the next or from one circumstance to the next. We don't know the details. We know only the security that God will keep us and never let us go. So, when we experience situations that are painful, infuriating, confusing, uncomfortable, threatening, and we wonder, does God keep me . . . ?

We can be sure that the answer is always YES.

Portrait of the author by Andrzej Bednarczyk, professor of painting at Akademia Sztuk Pieknych in Krakow, Poland, sketched during a lecture in Kazimierz in 1991.

HOW DO YOU KNOW THAT?

INTRODUCTION

WHAT ARE AUTHORITIES?

EPISTOMOLOGY IS NOT A DISEASE

THE FOUR CORNERS
    I   Bible (Revelation)
   II Rationality
  III Institution (Tradition)
  IV Experience

GETTING SQUARE
    Cheese or Beer?
    Preference in Religious Systems
    Your Epistemological Temperature
    The Well and Story Approach
    Seeing with a Single Eye

33 QUESTIONS
    Themes for Discussion
    with responses by Ellis Potter

■ ■ ■ ■

How do you know that?

When I asked this question as a child, I was told, 'You'll understand when you are older', or 'The Trinity is a paradox', or given some other vague response. It was frustrating to hear that kind of response. It didn't help me to trust the people I was asking. Much of my life has been a search for ways to answer *How do you know that?*—and to safely push the envelope of knowing. This book is the result of 67 years (so far) of pushing.

Like most people, you have probably asked *How do you know that?* many times in your life. How old were you when you first asked it? How old were you when someone first asked *you*? Many children start asking it at two or three years of age.

'How do you know that?' includes 'Who told you?' and 'What is your source for knowing it?' We all need to be secure about what we know. Different sources of knowledge are often in conflict or competition with each other in our lives and societies. Is this the way it should be?

Our identity and the meaning of our lives depend upon how we know. It can be confusing and stressful when different sources of knowledge are in competition with each other. How can we deal with this? Should we pick one source and reject the other? Should we free ourselves of authoritative sources of knowledge altogether?

In this book, we will explore some authoritative sources that inform our knowledge. In some ways, these sources are quite different from each other; in fact, they might seem as if they don't go together at all, or will compete with each other. But what if the different sources of authority actually *complete* or 'complement' each other? We will explore this possibility, in order to see how it may give us a richer and fuller understanding of our lives and the world.

WHAT ARE AUTHORITIES?

What are the authorities in your life? When I pose this question to groups of people, I usually get a long and unpredictable list of answers. Here is a sample:

> Parents
> God
> Police
> Government
> Teachers
> Peers
> Friends
> Myself
> The Law
> Gravity
> Celebrities
> Experience
> Media
> Advertisers
> Food
> Family
> Nation
> Mental Faculties
> Senses
> Science
> Moral Values
> Pastor
> Encyclopedia
> Bible
> Feelings
> Weather
> The Devil

What do all of these examples of authority have in common? In other words, what *is* authority? Some people say 'influence'. Others say, 'a source of truth'. Many people say, 'Authority is something that you give to someone or something', although that doesn't seem to work. For instance, you can't 'give' authority to gravity, because gravity just has it. Some things and some people have authority whether we give it or not. They have authority before we were born. The idea that authority is inherent in some things does not mean that the authority is friendly or convenient to us. If you fall off a building, gravity won't cooperate to save your life.

Often people think of authority as 'power'. But they don't mean something like electricity; they are talking about power in human relationships. Authority seems to include both personal and impersonal aspects. Most people also realize that authority is necessary for life, although it can be misused or misapplied. If I were to put it in my own words, I would define authority like this:

Authority is the power to describe reality.

How can we understand this? How can we apply this to real life? Think of parents and children. Parents are an authority for young children, because parents have the power to describe reality for children. They describe bedtime, playtime, and diet for children. They describe where children can play—in the backyard or in the garden, but not in the busy street.

Very young children cannot describe reality for themselves and need the authority of their parents for survival. They don't have the necessary vision or the scope of experience. Their lives depend on the authority of their parents. They may die if they play in the street rather than in the garden.

We also know that parents don't always exercise authority perfectly. During childhood we were all, to some extent, distorted and wounded and squashed by our fathers and mothers, because they made mistakes in exercising their authority. Still, insofar as children cannot describe reality for themselves, they must depend on their parents. There's no way around it.

It isn't only little children who need authority. People of all ages need the authority of the law and government and society and family and economic structures, in order to be safe from chaos and death.

Doctors are another example of authority. A doctor has the power to describe illness and health to the patient. A doctor can say, 'This is your disease, this is why you are sick, and here is the medication you need to cure the sickness.' In many cases a patient will die if they refuse the authority of the doctor. And just as there are imperfect parents, there are imperfect doctors. Sometimes you get a doctor who is incompetent, in which case his authority may be unhelpful and even dangerous. Occasionally, a doctor may only prescribe medication X, because he knows that the company that manufactures medication

X will reward him with a luxurious holiday if he sells enough bottles of X.

As you can see by these examples of human authority, there is no guarantee that the authority will *describe* reality accurately. The authority simply describes it. We hope that the description is accurate, but sometimes it isn't. There's an element of trust in living with authority. Trusting means taking a risk and believing there will be a benefit to a relationship of authority, rather than harm. Interpersonal authority functions best when there is trust.

Advertisers have the authority to describe the reality of pleasure and beauty and health to the public. They have the power to tell us how to identify ourselves: how to be acceptable, and wanted, and envied, and influential, and admired. Advertisers have the power to convince us that buying and using a variety of products will give us a good identity and fulfillment.

Authority is connected with the word 'auto', which means 'self', as in 'automobile' and 'autobiography'. But if authority is related to the 'self', which self should we start with? Should we start with 'myself'? Does that mean I have to be a God for myself? Am I good at being God? Or might 'self' refer to a powerful other self, or a trusted other self? Should the other self be God?

Here is another question involving the 'auto' of authority: What do we call a person who writes a book? We call him an 'author'. An author has the authority to describe the reality in the book.

If Mary writes a novel, she might write, 'John is an alcoholic.' When George reads the book, he might say, 'I don't think John is an alcoholic. It's not fair or nice to call John an alcoholic.' How do you think Mary will respond? If she is like most authors, then she'll probably say, 'My dear George, you're completely crazy because I am the author of my book and I can say whatever I want. If I say that John is green with five legs, then he's green with five legs. To this book I am God.' That's an author's authority. The author of a book has the power to describe the reality in the book however he or she wants.

The way people use authority can be good or bad or smart or stupid, a blessing or a curse, but in each case it involves the power to describe what the world is like.

There are many kinds of authority in the world. The focus of this book is the authoritative sources that inform our knowledge—our knowledge about anything. What has authority to help us to *know truly?*

EPISTEMOLOGY IS NOT A DISEASE

What is *epistemology*? It's not a disease. It's the study of how we know, and how we know we know. Epistemology has its roots in the Greek words for 'knowledge' and 'study of', so it's about how we comprehend and contextualize our information. It's about how we process and relate to information and experiences.

Epistemology is a very ordinary thing. It happens every day, and in quite different ways. For example, do you know that you like chocolate? If you do, then how do you know that? Do you have to discuss it with somebody before you know you like it? Do you have to read a book to figure out that you like it? Do you have to work out a mathematical equation to know that you like it?

No. You know that you like it by experience. You put the chocolate in your mouth, and you experience pleasure, and you know. This knowledge is not open to discussion. If you tell me, 'I like chocolate', and if I doubt that, then I'm being silly.

The Romans had a proverb: 'De gustibus non est disputandum.' This means, 'Taste is not debatable.' It is rooted in experience. Similarly, if you tell me that your favorite color is red, it's ridiculous for me to say, 'That is wrong, it should be blue', or to say, 'Don't you want to change it to blue?' Experience cannot be disputed, although the meaning of it can.

How about this: Do you know that two plus two equals four? How do you know that? Some people say that their teacher once told them that two plus two equals four. But the teacher could not have told them all the combinations of numbers that could be added. We learn a rational process of knowing how numbers combine and fit together. Rational means experiencing reality in 'ratios', which are relationships.

You know that two plus two equals four, but you don't know what it tastes like. So your knowledge of two plus two is different from your knowledge of chocolate. Which is the more true knowledge? They are equally true, but very different.

Do you know that you stop at the red light and go at the green light? How do you know that? Many people say that that knowledge is logical. But it isn't. Red is a hot, active color, and it means 'go'. Ask any bull or bee. Green is a cool, quiet color. It means rest. Ask any interior decorator. Our knowledge about the red light and the green light is not logical; it is traditional or cultural. It is true, necessary and life-saving knowledge. Even if this knowledge is not rational, it wouldn't be wise to ignore it. We need this kind of knowledge in order to live our lives. It is a deeply set custom and rhythm for our lives. That red means stop and green means go has become a given for pedestrians and motor vehicle drivers. We might get into an accident and die if we disregarded it. Cultural and traditional knowledge is different from experiential and rational knowledge, but equally true.

Do you know that your friend likes you? How do you know that? Perhaps they tell you. Maybe they don't avoid you. They might laugh at your jokes and try to encourage you. This knowledge can be subtle, but it can also be very strong. We need this kind of knowledge in our lives.

Do you know that the Bible, or Koran, or Upanishads, or Torah, or some other holy book, is true? How do you know that? You might know it because of its historical veracity, or its internal consistency, or its healthy application to your own life. Your knowledge that the Bible or another holy book is true is also going to include faith—in a similar way that you need a degree of faith to know that your friend likes you.

As you can see by these examples, there are many different ways of knowing. Are there other examples that you can think of? Knowing is rich and complex—so much so that we cannot have a total controlling grasp of knowing. We cannot see the whole picture from the point of view of any one way of knowing. We don't know what everything tastes like, and not everything has a taste; and not all of our knowledge is logical. And yet the different ways of knowing belong together in a full and lively epistemology. The relationship between these different kinds of knowing should not be competition, but complementarity. That means that they need and complete each other.

The Four Corners

Now let's look at the different *sources* that inform our knowing. To begin with, imagine a square. Each of the corners will represent an authoritative source that informs our knowledge or epistemology.

We'll explore each of these corners individually, as well as their relationship to each other, and see why all of them are needed for a full epistemology.

THE FIRST CORNER

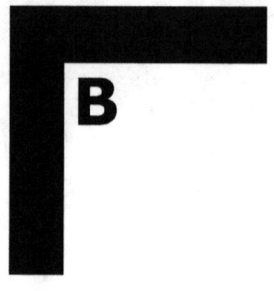

The first corner is labelled **B** for **Bible** (or Revelation). The Bible, or other revelations like the Koran, Upanishads, and Vedas, tell us things about reality that we could not know in any other way. For instance, the Bible tells us that reality is not mechanical, but fundamentally personal, beginning with a God who is a Trinity of three Persons. This information, if true, could not be determined by science or rationality. It could not be discovered by observation of the physical world or by laboratory experimentation. It is revelatory knowledge. Of course, such information should not conflict with science or rationality; it should complement what we learn on the basis of science and rationality. But the information itself cannot be obtained scientifically.

Revelation means information that comes from the supernatural into the natural world. As an example, consider information itself. It is widely understood, especially in the field of biology, that information (i.e., the genetic code) governs the functioning of the material of life. Although information obviously exists and controls matter, there is no evidence that matter *produces* information. In trying to understand this, the most reasonable hypothesis or assumption is that information is supernatural. The more religious hypothesis is that matter *does* produce information, and we have faith that the process will eventually be discovered. The religion of this hypothesis is 'scientism', or the belief that science can discover all truth (based on the unproven assumption that matter comprises all of reality). But this kind of faith seems rather extreme. Science is a wonderful gift, but worshipping it is not a good idea.

THE SECOND CORNER

The second corner is labelled **R** for **Rationality**. As I mentioned earlier, rationality means seeing reality in ratios, or relationships. Understanding ratios or relationships involves logic; such understanding can generally be expressed mathematically.

We learn things about reality from our rationality that we cannot learn from the Bible or other revelations. For instance, as a result of rationality, dental science has developed. The Bible makes no mention of dentistry. Someone who wants their knowledge to be informed only by the Bible (or the Revelation corner in general) might not ever go to the dentist, because dentistry is extra-biblical knowledge. However, knowledge of dentistry is one way of obeying the biblical command to have dominion over creation. We should not 'go with the flow' of tooth decay, but have dominion over it. In this way, dentistry is not in conflict with what we learn from the Bible, but is in a complementary (or completing) relationship with the Bible. It brings us a more full understanding of the world.

Rationality also gives people dominion over the rest of creation. Civilization requires the manipulation of nature, according to the rational imagination of people. For example, wheat naturally grows along stream banks, mixed with many other plants. Human civilization requires human beings to say to the wheat, 'You will grow only in this field, and no other plants will grow here.' This is not how wheat naturally behaves. This happens because a supernatural source of rational, imaginative, and creative power, is imposed on the wheat. If human beings did not manipulate nature in this rational and creative way, then society would never be possible. We would have to go back to living as hunters and gatherers. At the same time, this domination of nature must include careful husbandry and preservation, or there won't be any nature left to work with.

If the relationship between rationality and revelation is complementary, it means both corners are essential and neither corner is adequate. There are also ways in which they interrelate. If God has created the world, then we can find out many things about the Creator by examining the creation. The creation is beautiful, orderly, faithful, and dependable; and God invites us to observe all of this, to better understand Him. The more we discover through archeology, molecular biology, quantum physics, and other disciplines that depend upon reason, the more we know about God and His work.

THE THIRD CORNER

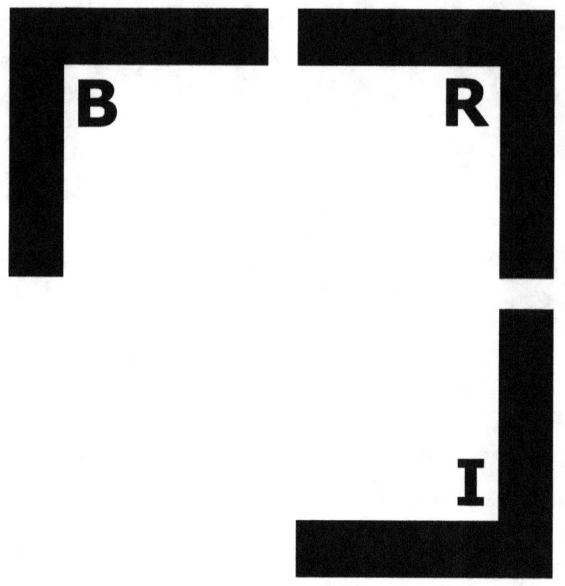

The lower right corner **I** represents **Institution**, or tradition, the third authoritative source that informs our knowledge.

Institution means various groups of people living together over time. It includes marriage, family, friendship, community, nation, church, and other situations where people are in relationship with each other. All institutions develop traditions, which help us to build and preserve our knowledge, so that each generation does not need to reinvent the wheel. Some traditions are short-lived and others last longer.

We learn things from institutions that we don't learn from rationality or by revelation. Knowledge gained through institution cannot be expressed mathematically. Institution brings us knowledge through relationships between people.

The revelation of the Bible (e.g., 1 John 4:19-21) tells us that we can only know God and His love by loving each other. We can only love each other in institutions. We cannot know this love by doing a religious ceremony. We cannot know it by just feeling it either. Love is not a feeling. Love is a series of responsible choices that promote and encourage the other so that they can become who God intends them to be. The purpose of love is to make us more fully real. As you can see, love is not self-centered. The center of love, the focus of love, is the other person. So the purpose of love is not to express my satisfaction or my desire or my enjoyment. The purpose of love is not to gratify myself, or even to gratify the other. The purpose of love is to establish people in truth. For this reason, love can sometimes be experienced as difficult or painful.

Many people feel that they know the love of God when they experience people loving them. This is half of the truth. This is love that we receive, or get. The other half of the truth is that we know the love of God by loving other people sacrificially. This is the love that we do. The relationship between getting and doing should be complementary rather than competitive.

We cannot know love only by reading the Bible. We cannot know love by reason. We have to live out this love in relationships, in institutions. In the Old Testament, the Hebrew word for 'know' means sexual intercourse. That's not something you do rationally at a distance. It's a committed, engaged, involved way of knowing.

We should not think that we can go and live in a cave with our Bible and know God in all the ways we need to. It doesn't work like that in the biblical worldview. The Bible tells us that we need to live in relationships, families, churches, cultures, and nations. Knowing God includes loving others within these institutions.

Of course, knowing by and through the institution or tradition can be exaggerated or confused. Sometimes people say, 'We know this is true because we have always done it this way.' Or, 'This is true because we have always believed it.' Or, an elderly church member who is disturbed by modern translations of the Bible may say, 'If the King James version was good enough for the apostle Paul, it is good enough for me.' This kind of thinking removes the corner **I** from the necessary context of the other corners.

Our understanding of the Christian faith was deepened through the various early church councils and historical developments within the church. These institutions gave us increasing definition and refinement of the truth as expressed in the Bible. An example of this refinement is the Nicene Creed, which begins like this: 'We believe in one God, the Father Almighty, Maker of heaven and earth, and of all things visible and invisible. And in one Lord Jesus Christ, the only-begotten Son of God....'

There is nothing in the Nicene Creed that you won't find in the Bible. The Creed was developed by a group of people who gathered and wanted to find a way to express key ideas from the Bible. The Creed is a product of that gathering, of those people who came together in prayer and conversation and Scripture reading. The Creed adds definition and refinement to our understanding of God and the Christian faith. It focuses believers on central aspects of the truth, while also preventing heresies from entering into people's understanding of God. The Creed doesn't alter anything that the Bible says—it doesn't reinvent the wheel, doesn't reinvent the truth—but reflects and distills the truth.

The Nicene Creed is an example of knowledge that comes to us through community or institutions. We know about God by living in the historical institution of the church. We know by the giving, submitting, and mutually supportive relationships of the community of His people.

Many of us have suffered in churches from bad leaders, prejudice, bigotry, abuse, rejection, manipulation, or tyranny. We might be tempted to eliminate the church because of these problems; but that would be like throwing out the proverbial baby with the bathwater. The institution needs to be part of the mix of how we live in reality and know reality.

There is another, deeper way of seeing the importance of relationships in epistemology. It is the realization that fact does not equal truth. Truth is fact plus meaning. What does meaning mean? Meaning means relationships, which means that nothing has meaning in itself. For instance, the meaning of the color red is not in the color red. It is in its relationships with green, and blue, and other colors. The meaning of Adam in the creation account of the Bible was not in himself but in his relationships with God and with Eve. The meaning of Jesus is not in Jesus but in his relationship with the Father and the Holy Spirit. The meaning of you is not in you but in your relationships with others. All true knowledge is relational in a variety of ways.

THE FOURTH CORNER

The fourth corner **E** stands for **Experience**. Our personal experience is essential for understanding reality. We need to experience awe, fear, sorrow, hope, comfort, and thankfulness because we don't get them from the other corners. Personal experiences are subjective, meaning that they depend upon your point of view, which is unique. But the fact that they are subjective does not mean that they are untrue. There are objective and subjective parts of truth, which are both essential. Actually, we find that there is no objective truth, and there is no subjective truth. All true truth is always both objective and subjective. The true and lively relationship between the objectivity and subjectivity of truth should be complementary rather than competitive.

If four people witness an automobile accident from different vantage points, what they see, or subjectively experience, is going to be different from each other. Their experiences of the accident should not compete with each other but complement each other to give a truer knowledge of what happened. Some literary critics of the Four Gospels would want us to believe that because there is not only one objective experience of the accident but several subjective experiences, the accident never happened. The accident happened, and Jesus objectively happened. There are subjective views of both.

Personal experience is an authoritative source of knowledge about reality. We each have individual, subjective, 'unshareable' experiences of nature, humanness, love, healing, knowledge, guidance, imagination, intuition, and reality as a whole. All of these experiences inform our epistemology. We learn things through those personal experiences that we don't learn through reading the Bible. We don't learn those things by thinking and reasoning. We don't learn them from institutions.

Christians know that God loves them because He comforts them. He thrills them. He gives them joy and fills their hearts with wonder and the Holy Spirit. God is a personal and relational God, and so a person's knowledge of God cannot be at a distance. It must be very intimate. It will be unique for each person. It's like a marriage: I could not share the deep experiences of my marriage with you, any more than you could share your experience of marriage with me. And yet the experience is essential for us to truly know marriage.

However, although experience is necessary, it can't be isolated from the other corners. If I depend only on my experience to know reality, I'm living in an experience bubble. In that case, I would need to say, 'God *is* my experience.' But if God isn't more than my experience, then I am worshipping myself, which is totally self-referential. This is not Christianity. It is humanism or self-ism; it forces you to be your own God.

GETTING SQUARE

Each of the four corners is a different authority for our knowledge of reality. Each corner is *unique*, in the sense that it tells us something that the other corners cannot. Each corner is *essential*, in the sense that we cannot understand God and the whole of reality if we leave any of the corners out of the epistemology.

We need all four corners. We cannot know reality truly if we only have our rationality. We cannot know reality truly if we only have the authority and tradition of the community. We cannot know reality truly if we sit in a room and read a holy book all day. If we have only personal experience, and we see angels and make prophecies, but don't have the other corners to complete our understanding of reality, then our personal experience is not enough—and may even be dangerous.

In fact, all of the corners, if isolated, can be dangerous. But that does not mean we can live without them. Our rationality is not safe, if that is all we focus on, because it can disconnect us from our emotions, our intuitions, and our imagination. The institution is not safe either. The church, for instance, can become manipulative or strongly associated with the state. The Bible isn't safe either, if isolated from the other corners, because in order to understand reality fully we also need our reason, our experiences, and the institutions and traditions of the community to contextualize our reading of Scripture.

Sometimes people want to know, 'Which of the corners is most important? Which one takes precedence over the others?' But the four corners are not a hierarchy. No one is higher than another. They are a complementarity, meaning that all are necessary for understanding reality. There is no one corner that dominates all the others. They are not equal in function, nor are they interchangeable. They are all essential and distinct and unique. None of them are dependent, and none of them is first. They're all primary and all original.

Cheese or Beer: Which do you prefer?

People sometimes call the lecture which is the basis for this book the *Cheese Lecture*, because if you start with the **B** corner of the square, and move in a clockwise direction, the first letter of each corner spells *brie*, a French cheese. If you start in the **B** corner and move counterclockwise, the letters almost spell *bier* in German. So you can have either beer or cheese. It is evidently a nutritious and inviting subject.

I once gave this talk in Switzerland, and an evangelical Bible scholar responded with the following comment: 'You need to redraw your diagram with the Bible on top, so that it trickles down over everything else, or else you need to put the Bible on the bottom, so it's the foundation of everything.' On a personal level as a pastor, I tended to agree with him. But I don't trust my natural tendency in this regard. Actually, I don't trust a lot of my natural tendencies. If I'm a sinner, if I'm broken and confused, if I'm distorted, then I should *expect* my view to be out of focus. That may not be an encouraging thing to say, but it's a real thing to say. I should expect my natural desires and tendencies and prejudices to be out of focus and out of kilter. So I have to make a deliberate effort to step back from my natural preferences, looking from a wider perspective than just myself. Only then do I start to see that all of the four corners are essential for a true and adequate epistemology.

Everybody has a favorite corner. We naturally feel that our strongest corner is the most true corner, and the corner that should govern all of the other corners. When we lean strongly enough toward one corner, we can develop an extremism or fanaticism. As a result, our epistemology becomes distorted and incomplete.

Stress, misunderstanding and confusion can arise when people favour one corner over another. Where do these preferences come from? Sometimes they're shaped by our personality and upbringing. Sometimes we inhale them from the cultural atmosphere in which we live. Sometimes preferences are inspired by our ignorance and blind spots. We may avoid or fear or downplay a corner because we don't know anything about it, or because we had a bad experience in that corner, or were manipulated in that corner, or suffered a failure or frustration in that corner—or because our Mom and Dad said negative things about that corner.

Sometimes, scientists discount the Bible because of their extreme emphasis on rationality. Christians may discount rationality because of their extreme emphasis on faith. It is only natural to want to strengthen what is strong, but we need to be careful about that natural tendency.

The apostle Paul was not afraid of his weaknesses. Before he was a Christian, while still a member of the Pharisee party, Paul was strong in a legalistic understanding of truth. After he became a Christian, various physical, social, and emotional experiences weakened his legalism, and consequently he developed a stronger and fuller epistemology. In his second letter to the Corinthians, Paul tells the reader, 'For when I am weak, then I am strong' (2 Corinthians 12:10). When Paul was strong in one corner, he was naturally strong. When this natural tendency became 'weaker', his epistemology became fuller and more spiritually strong—that is, more real and inclusive of the whole of reality.

Maybe we can think here of 'Judo' epistemology. 'Judo' is the 'gentle way', which gives way, falls back and uses an opposing force to shape reality. When we insist on the primacy of our favorite corner and are strong in it, our understanding of truth will be weak. When we fall back, and consider the surprising strength and validity of our non-favorite corners, our understanding of truth will be strengthened.

If we strengthen what is strong, we actually become weaker in our understanding of reality. If we strengthen what is weak, we become fuller, richer, and stronger in our epistemology. It's hard to accept this advice, because it requires humility, trust and faith—because we don't see the value of the weak things in life. We walk by sight in the area of strength, while we also need to walk by faith in the area that is weak. I find it exceedingly difficult to take that advice, and to actually deliberately strengthen what is weak. Approaching our weakness can make us feel quite vulnerable, and yet it is through this vulnerability that we can grow in our understanding and strength.

Preference in Religious Systems

The tendency to focus on a particular corner isn't only a problem with individuals. It happens in religious systems as a whole. The Bible corner can be overemphasized, to the exclusion of other corners, in evangelical forms of Christianity. The Bible can become the center of everything, marginalizing the importance of relationships, experience, and rationality. A similar overemphasis on a text can occur in certain forms of Judaism (Torah), Islam (Koran), and Mormonism (The Book of Mormon). In all of these instances, people may understand God and reality totally on the basis of a particular revelatory text. As I mentioned earlier, as an evangelical Christian I naturally tend to emphasize the **B** corner, but I have to be careful about that, and to avoid assuming that what I naturally prefer is the basic truth of human life.

In some worldviews, people tend to gravitate toward the rationality corner at the expense of the other three corners. Examples of such worldviews include atheistic humanism and communism. Both of these approaches tend to ignore or diminish human experience, and often try to work out the truth mathematically or scientifically. That is why, under the old communist regimes, writers and teachers were sometimes referred to as 'engineers of the human soul'.

Liberal branches of Christianity lean toward the rationality corner. Some liberal churches are hyper-intellectual, and will sift Bible content through an intellectual grid in order to shape it in a way that better fits the **R** corner. Many of these churches will attempt to strip away any supernatural or faith elements of Scripture and place them within the context of naturalistic explanations.

Great and exclusive strength in the rational corner can actually produce an epistemological weakness and incompleteness. Several years ago I was in Cluj-Napoca/Kolozsvár, the capital of Transylvania. A Christian café called Quo Vadis was having a series of open discussion evenings and I was invited to lead one. The Quo Vadis was decorated in early post-postmodern style and was one of the most interesting places in the city. About a dozen people gathered around a large, beautiful Art Nouveauish glass-topped table. Half of them were Christians and half were not. Their professions included teacher, nurse, psychologist, architect, historian and brain surgeon.

The Christians were the hosts and began the conversation with talk about the nature of faith, what to expect in answer to prayers, and experiences of the supernatural.

After about thirty minutes of this a man suddenly erupted in excellent English: 'Oh, you Christians with your experiences! I am a brain surgeon and can produce all your visions, emotions and sensations of what you call the supernatural surgically, electronically and chemically. There is no supernatural or God. There is only matter and energy in reality.' He went on with examples and illustrations for quite a while. I was listening and praying at the same time, asking for wisdom to answer this man. When he finally stopped, I surprised myself by saying, 'You speak as a man who has never been in love.' He froze and his face started to turn red. I asked, '*Are* you in love?' He said, 'Yes, I am.' I asked him, 'Can you reproduce your relationship with this woman in your laboratory and surgery—and does she know this?'

There was a long pause and then he said, 'You got me.' He was experiencing an epistemological paradigm shift. He saw the light. He could see that he could not reduce his experiences of life to matter and energy, but he wanted to reduce other peoples' experiences. He was a refreshingly honest and open person, and therefore probably an excellent scientist. He had been putting so much weight on the **R** or rationality corner that his epistemology was lopsided and distorted. The other three corners had been invalidated by his exclusive investment in the **R** corner. He seemed to be positive about broadening his epistemological base.

Other religious systems focus on the Institution corner. They overemphasize tradition, and are quite often nationalistic. Examples include certain versions of Shinto and Judaism. Within Christianity, Orthodox and Catholic churches may also tend toward the **I** or institution (tradition) corner. Protestants would tend to say that the Bible describes the church, and that in order to know what the church should be like, we need to begin with the Bible. They would have an epistemological hierarchy that looks like this:

God

Bible

Church

Orthodox believers believe the church wrote the Bible. Therefore, their epistemological hierarchy is:

God

Church

Bible

This means that the Bible must be understood within the Holy Tradition of Holy Mother Church.

Catholics tend toward an equal emphasis on Bible and Institution. They have a more open view of the revelatory activity of the Holy Spirit, in that they believe the Spirit continues to inspire the church. Catholics would have an epistemological hierarchy that looks something like this:

God

Bible + Church

I once spoke at the Gdansk Naval Academy in Poland, where all of the officer candidates were Catholic. They were on their feet shouting when I presented the four squares as all equal and necessary, because in their view I had insulted Holy Mother Church for not making Institution the foundation of all the other squares. I sympathized with their frustration, insofar as I agree that Institution is essential; it cannot be ignored or pushed into the background. But the other corners are also essential. If we say that any one corner is a derivative of one of the others, or a subsidiary of one of the others, then we will fight wars over which one is primary—and we *have* fought wars over which one is primary. But if we recognize that they are all essential, and their relationship is complementary rather than derivative or competitive, we will find a stability and peace and completeness.

Personal experience of reality is also an essential part of a full and healthy epistemology. However, some religious systems focus excessively on the experience corner. Examples include some forms of Hinduism and Buddhism, and New Age religions. Some forms of Pentecostal or charismatic Christianity also lean toward this corner. People in these kinds of churches sometimes understand the Bible not in terms of what it says, but in terms of how they experience what it says. This tendency would also be to some extent true of a postmodern reading of a text, in which the meaning of a text is the reader's response to the text.

Again, it is common that people tend to emphasize what comes naturally to them. A person with a sharp mind goes to the rationality corner, and might neglect or mistrust the experience corner. A person with strong life experiences might be drawn toward the experience corner, and be blessed by the experiences; they might then continue to move into this corner, to the point of neglecting or mistrusting the rationality corner—and then we would have the opposite problem. It's not a worse problem, it's just the opposite problem. This problem can and does occur in how people deal with all of the corners.

Your Epistemological Temperature

On your own, or with a group of people, consider the following questions about each of the four corners:

- What is your preferred corner for understanding truth?

- Does your personality play any role in this preference? For example, are you very emotional or in touch with your inner experiences? Or are you more rational and analytically minded?

- What aspect of truth was rewarded and encouraged when you were growing up?

- What aspect of truth was discouraged or punished?

- What aspect of truth was overlooked or ignored?

- What aspect of truth was considered dangerous?

- Currently, which corner or corners do you avoid or dislike?

- Which corner or corners do you try to control using your favorite corner?

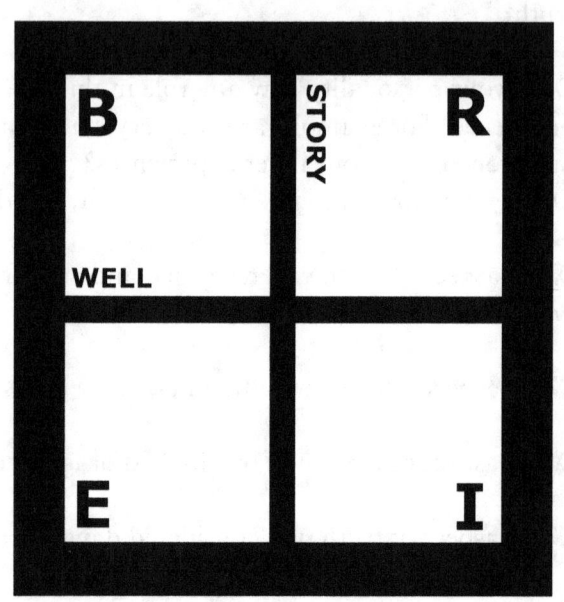

The Well and Story Approach

You may have noticed two axes across the center of our epistemology square—a horizontal line and a vertical line dividing up the square. These two axes will help us form an additional picture for understanding epistemology.

Let's name the two axes: we'll call one axis 'well' (like a water well) and the other axis 'story'. The well axis refers to a way of understanding revelatory texts, such as the Bible, Koran, or Torah. This approach involves drawing out what we need from a text, as we might draw water from a well. We put in our bucket and draw out data, guidance, comfort, inspiration, correction, rebuke, promises, and anything else that we might need. We know reality through actively engaging with it and experiencing its effect on us and our reaction to it.

In contrast, the story approach refers to a way of understanding that involves being aware of the overall frame of reality. This approach focuses on large historical sweeps of civilization or culture, or on the history of God's activity and intention as expressed in a text. The story approach places us and our experiences in the big picture, and allows us to know where we are and what we *mean*. This is perhaps a more passive approach of allowing the reality outside of ourselves to be what it is.

What is the center and focus of the well approach? It's me. What is the center and focus of the story approach? It's God or reality as a whole. People often wonder which of these two areas of focus matters more. They ask, 'Which is more important?' Can you see how wrong that question is? It's like somebody asking you which side of a coin you would like to have. You have to have both sides. A real coin that has value has two sides.

If the Bible is true, God made us to be significant people with subjective points of view. That means we should not only focus on God when reading the Bible, and pretend that we are irrelevant or don't exist. If God made us, then we must not discount ourselves. Our needs and our point of view matter.

However, if we just choose the well approach—ignoring the story approach—that makes experience our only teacher and disconnects us from the reality outside of ourselves. Without the context of the story approach, which is about God, we are alienated and isolated, because we are decontextualized from the whole of reality. The Bible is the story of God. It's the story of His character and activity in history. If we read the Bible without this framework, then we are not in a true relationship with God, who is greater than our subjective experience. Without this framework, there is no meaning in what we are reading—in fact, there is no meaning in anything—because meaning *means* relationships. Meaning, as I mentioned earlier, depends on a relationship to something outside of ourselves. Nothing has meaning in itself. If I isolate myself and only have the well approach, I have less and less meaning.

We are often confronted with questions that invite and challenge us to choose the well approach over the story approach, or the story approach over the well approach. But answering such questions can be destructive. We need both approaches in the same way that we need both sides of a coin to have a 'real' coin.

Let's put the well and story approaches into two columns, as shown below:

WELL	STORY

Now let's consider some contrasting pairs of words and ideas. We are going to place one of the pair under 'well' and the other under 'story'.

WELL	STORY
Subjective	Objective
Freedom	Form
Wife	Husband
Diversity	Unity
Mystery	Definition
Right-brain	Left-brain
Microscope	Telescope
Share my Faith	Share the Faith
My Testimony	Testimony of Jesus
Wave	Particle
Yin	Yang
Free Will	Predestination
Jesus as Man	Christ as God
Non-accurate Truth	Accurate Truth
Mercy	Justice
Educating	Teaching
Art	Science
Apophatic	Cataphatic
Deductive	Inductive
Grace	Law

In the chart to the left you see the elements of many pairs assigned to the 'well' or 'story' column. Look at each pair and reflect on it. What do you think? Do you think that any of the items is on the wrong side? Why? Some of the pairs may be more obvious than others. You may wish to share this exercise with other people, and see how they would place the items.

The first pair is 'subjective' and 'objective'. Most people can see that 'subjective', which relates to me or the viewer, goes in the well column; and that 'objective', which relates to that part of reality which is independent of me, goes in the story column. Following on from the complementarity of the four-cornered square, we see that the relationship between objective and subjective should not be competition but complementarity. Again, the question about choosing between them is destructive, because we need them both.

Now consider this pair: 'freedom' and 'form'. We can see that 'form' belongs in the story column, because it involves the general frame of reality. General forms would include, for instance, the laws of gravity and thermodynamics. On the other hand, 'freedom' belongs in the well column, and represents the infinite variety of choices and activity that are given meaning by the structure of the form. Again, both freedom and form are essential; they should not compete with each other.

The next pair is 'wife' and 'husband'. 'Wife' is more on the well side. The wife is a source (or well) of life. Life is born out of the wife. The wife is more like home, mother, comfort, intimacy, and unconditional acceptance. 'Husband' is more on the story side, because he provides a protecting context for the flourishing of the well. But which is more important in a marriage? The obvious answer is that they are equally important. But the relationship is not 50-50. If you take away the wife, you don't have 50% of a marriage left, because a marriage is 100% the wife. It is also 100% the husband. Marriage is a 200% reality—which is also true of our relationship with God. (Actually, a physicist has pointed out to me that the 100% of the wife is not added to the 100% of the husband, but multiplied by 100%. That would give us a 10,000% reality, making marriage a rich and complex thing indeed.)

The next pair is 'diversity and 'unity'. What do you think? Into which column will you put each of them? Why? What about 'mystery and 'definition? Where will they go?

For each pair, which side is 'more true'? The answer is neither. Both are equally true, and both are needed for a full truth. For example, as we have said, both 'wife' and 'husband' are needed for the full truth of marriage. The two should not relate to each other in competition but in complementarity. This complementarity depends on the wife and husband being different from each other and not identical.

Let's take a closer look at another pair. Consider the pair 'my faith' and 'the faith'. In many Christian groups one mostly hears about sharing 'my faith', but not much about sharing 'the faith'. In order to bring this pair into a whole and balanced focus, I like to ask people the question, 'Who is Jesus Christ before you were born?' This question is difficult for people who concentrate on the well approach to reality. They know how they feel about Jesus, and what they have experienced of Jesus in their own lives; but they might not have learned much, through the story approach, about who Jesus is independent of their experiences. They can speak more about their unique experiences of Jesus than they can about the objective reality of Jesus—which can actually be shared. It is more possible to share 'the faith' than 'my faith'. We all share and know together the facts about Jesus; our experiences of Jesus are more private and more difficult to share.

On the other hand, there are people who know a great deal about Jesus but don't have any actual experience with Jesus. This leans too far on the story side and doesn't make a complete reality either.

Notice that some parts of reality don't fit in the well and story columns. 'Good' and 'evil' are not presented as a pair because, in the biblical worldview, good and evil are not two complementary aspects of truth or equal opposites. Good is the original reality; evil is a derivative distortion. Only good is true; evil is false. This view is in contrast with dualistic worldviews, in which 'good' and 'evil' are both regarded as equally original in reality, and equally important in comprising truth.

For the same reason, the columns do not include the pairs 'love' and 'hate', or 'light' and 'darkness'—because, again, only the first member of each pair is true and original.

Finally, consider 'impersonal' and 'personal'. Do we exist in a reality that is fundamentally material and energetic with personal configurations—or a reality that is fundamentally personal, functioning in and out of a material and energetic matrix? If the Bible is true, then reality is fundamentally personal rather than mechanical or energetic. That is why the columns do not include the pair 'personal' and 'impersonal'; only 'personal' is true.

Seeing with a Single Eye

In our exploration of the four epistemology corners, we saw that people tend to have a favorite corner. The same is true of the well and story columns. People who value experiences will probably prefer the well column, whereas people who value reason and rationality will probably emphasize the story column. Most of us will have a natural tendency for one column over the other. Again, my advice is to strengthen what is weak, and bring a balance and wholeness into your approach to reality.

As we pray and work on strengthening our weaknesses, we will begin to see reality in a way that is more whole and complete. We will begin to experience a fuller living knowledge, rather than a partial knowledge. The process will be challenging and at times frightening, because it will involve a paradigm shift, or change in our model of reality. It will take us out of our comfort zone.

In the Sermon on the Mount, there is a little section where Jesus teaches about two areas of conflict in human life: investing and serving. He says (Matthew 6:19-21, 24):

Do not store up for yourselves treasures on earth, where moths and vermin destroy, and where thieves break in and steal. But store up for yourselves treasures in heaven, where moths and vermin do not destroy, and where thieves do not break in and steal. For where your treasure is, there your heart will be also...No one can serve two masters. Either you will hate the one and love the other, or you will be devoted to the one and despise the other. You cannot serve both God and money.

We are encouraged to invest ourselves in the total reality of heaven, which includes the earth, rather than investing in the limited, isolated and unviable context of the creation alone. We are encouraged to serve the Giver and not the gifts. We need to serve the God who gives the capacity to produce wealth. In between these two areas of (apparent) conflict is a little and much misunderstood section about perspective. Jesus says (Matthew 6:22-23):

The eye is the lamp of the body. If your eyes are healthy, your whole body will be full of light. But if your eyes are unhealthy, your whole body will be full of darkness. If then the light within you is darkness, how great is that darkness!

Our perception (the eye) is the light source of our life. Most modern translations render verse 22 as 'if your eye is good' or 'sound' or 'healthy', but the original Greek word is 'single'. This means to have a united, comprehensive and complimentary view of reality as a whole. In this way the apparent conflicts of the surrounding sections about investment and service are resolved. When we see 'storing up' and 'serving' in this single way or with a 'holistic' focus, then the conflicts are resolved by contextualizing everything in the Kingdom of God. We experience producing wealth and serving people as part of our lives in God's Kingdom. Can you see a connection between this section of the Sermon on the Mount and the four corners of our epistemology square, and the two axes? If we hold the four corners and two columns in complementary focus, will we be more full of light?

Seeing with a 'single' eye can be challenging. It means bringing together aspects of reality that don't seem to fit together rationally. Rationality is important, but it can be overemphasized and cause distortions—even in the church. During the Enlightenment and the scientific revolution, when there emerged a strong faith that all truth can be expressed in numbers, people began to draw reality on flat surfaces, using circle graphs and bar graphs. All the divisions always added up to 100%.

The Bible doesn't divide things up that way, but even the church took on the principles of the world and began to try to understand truth through the world's glasses. As a result, Christians have tended to divide everything up in mathematical terms. For example, the reality of predestination and free will is sometimes laid out on a flat surface as a pie chart, and people try to divide the pie into parts that add up to 100%. Some people divide the pie into 50-50 halves, but that doesn't seem very honouring to God's sovereignty. Other people might say that the pie is divided into 51% God's sovereignty and 49% people's free will. This is also not satisfactory. Even if we say it should be divided into 99% God's sovereignty and 1% free will, it still does not satisfy. The most logical understanding is that God is 100% sovereign—which means that human beings are chess pieces—or that human free will is 100% free—which means that God is on a deistic holiday.

It seems to me that instead of squashing reality onto a two-dimensional pie chart, it might be better to think of a free will disc, and predestination disc. Both the free will disc and the predestination disc are 100%. The discs interface to form a three-dimensional sphere of reality. This sphere expresses a 200% reality—or, as I mentioned earlier, a 10,000% reality. God's sovereignty is total and complete, and human free will is total and complete. The relationship between the sovereignty of God and the free will of man is not competition if we see them as a three-dimensional model rather than a two-dimensional model.

Just as we must see predestination and free will with a 'single eye', we must also see other seeming divisions, differences, and contrasts as unified. When we read the Bible, the well approach and the story approach are both necessary to understanding the truth. If we want to understand God and absolute reality in the fullest way, we

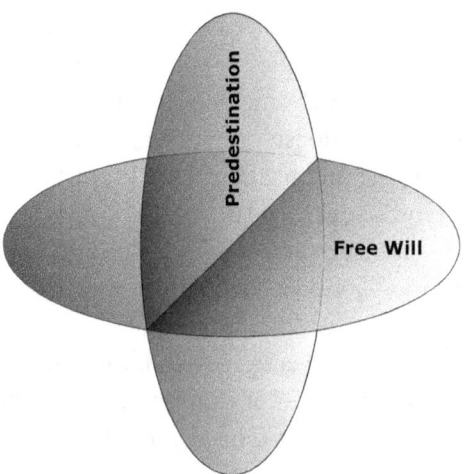

need to bring together all the major sources of this understanding, including the Bible, our experiences, rationality, and institutions or tradition. None of these stands above the others, and none of them can be left out.

The fact is that we are all unbalanced. We are all unhealthy. So the question is not, 'Am I unbalanced?' The question is, 'How am I unbalanced? How can I be healed?' We need to approach these challenges with humility.

Humility is not shyness or obsequiousness. Humility is realism. When I am realistic, I realize both my strengths and my weaknesses accurately. If I have a God-given strength for teaching, and I say, 'No, I'm sure I couldn't do that. I'm sure others could do it better'—that is not humility, it is pride. It is saying, 'God has made me with this strength, but I would feel better and people would think more highly of me, if I would deny it.' This looks like humility, but it isn't. It is creating myself according to the vanity of my own imagination. Real humility is accepting ourselves as we actually are, and not pretending to be strong or weak in ways that seem convenient to us.

Can we look at ourselves closely, and see our areas of distortion? Can we face our areas of distortion honestly, and through work and faith build a more comprehensive approach to our understanding of reality? It can take some effort. It makes life more complicated, and leaves us more vulnerable. But a complementary approach to truth makes our lives richer and fuller. It grounds us in reality and brings us into greater wholeness.   Amen.

33 QUESTIONS

These questions are taken from recordings of actual Q&A sessions after lectures and from readers of the lecture text. They have been only minimally edited, and therefore have a conversational rather than an academic or literary tone.

A real question helps us stop fluttering around a subject like moths and get to the heart of things. Only an ignorant question is a true question. It can be harder to ask good questions than to give good answers. What are your questions? Invest yourself in finding them.

1. *What are some of the obstacles that people face as they explore the Bible corner of epistemology?*

One obstacle is that people feel hurried. Sometimes Christians urge people to make a decision about the authority of the Bible without giving them time to think it through. People can feel pressure to understand everything about the Bible before they accept it as an authoritative source. Actually, we never understand any of the four sources fully. The Bible is perfect, but our understanding of it never is. So we shouldn't put pressure on ourselves to have a perfect understanding. People who believe that they have a perfect understanding of the Bible, or of any of the other sources of knowledge, sometimes become dangerous. My advice is to slow down. The search for truth is a *process* and it takes time.

Another common obstacle is that people are reluctant to accept the truth of the Christian faith unless they can prove that everything else is totally false. But I don't think that reflects reality. Buddhism doesn't need to be proven totally false in order for you to choose Jesus. Islam doesn't need to be proven totally false in order for you to be saved as a Christian. Other worldviews include some elements of truth, even if the worldviews as a whole don't adequately represent the absolute truth.

People also expect the Bible to be what it is not, and this too can be an obstacle. The Bible is not a science textbook, although what it says about reality does not conflict with science. Similarly, the Bible was written in other times and cultures, and sometimes people mistakenly expect it to speak directly to our time and culture in our terms.

2. *People with authority easily confuse having authority with having more worth and value. 'I've got the power, so I'm more important and superior.' Can you comment on this?*

Within God, the Father has authority and gives it to the Son; the Father commands and sends, and the Son obeys and goes. They are equally God. The same applies to the image of God—human beings. For example, parents have authority and children obey, but who is more human? They are both equally human. Having authority does not humanize a person, but rather has a specific function within human relationships.

Years ago, I was in communist East Germany in a church with about a hundred people. Most of them were farmers. I asked, 'Who is more human, the parents or the children?' They all said, 'The parents.' I was so shocked that I could barely catch my breath. I didn't know what to say. They were sure of their answer. There was no discussion. There was no speculation. That was reality for them. The parents were more human, the children were less human. And I thought to myself, 'I'm in a different culture now. I'm out of my box. How do I cope with this? What do I do?' I just had to move on. And these were Christians. I would call them, in my own egocentric way, Bible-believing Christians, but not Bible-understanding

Christians. They accepted the authority of the Bible as I do, and we were brothers, but I think they misunderstood something important. Fundamentally, we were together, but there were some ways that we were quite different.

Life is complex, even among Christians. We cannot expect all Christians to have the same cultural, political, economic, and social values and structures. Sometimes we will find ourselves in a culture, and our gut reaction will be, 'Oh, that's abnormal!'

But the real question is, 'Is it abnormal to God, or is it only abnormal to me?' If it's only abnormal to me, then I need to accept it. But if it's abnormal to God, if it's really outside His character and commands and the structure He gives for human life, then I need to say, 'There's a problem here. You're making a mistake, dear brother, and I feel called to persuade you of that.' But we have to be careful and humble, and really look to see whether we are speaking from cultural prejudice, or from a godly perspective.

3. *Can people under authority get confused about how to function in a relationship of authority?*

Sometimes people under authority want people with authority to take far more responsibility for their lives than they should. It can be very relaxing not to be responsible for your own life, and comforting to be dependent on others. But that would be a confused and wrong use of authority.

People under authority are sometimes victims. We tend to think of victims as innocent. In some ways, of course, they are, particularly in specific areas of victimization. But victims are people, and all people are guilty. No one should be reduced to being only a victim. Some people can manipulate reality through their victim status. Some feel that the meaning of life is to discover what life owes them, and to devote themselves to collecting. This is not how life actually works.

I often say, 'Without guilt there is no hope.' If we are only innocent victims, then all of our problems are caused by bad things that happen to us. In this case, the only hope is that better things will happen to us. But no one is promising us that better things will happen. If we are guilty, we need to be forgiven, and Someone is promising forgiveness.

4. Can you talk more about how freedom and form relate to authority?

I'll use the example of parents again. The authority of parents shapes the freedom of young children. Parents impose constraints in some areas of a child's life, but not in others. 'You can do *this*,' parents often say, 'but you can't do *that*.' Parents shape freedom in this way so that the children can live, safely and fully; in other words, the freedom that parents offer is a freedom that has form. It's not a shifting cloud of freedom, or a willy-nilly kind of freedom. A freedom without form is dangerous.

I offer you an equation:

Total freedom = Death

That's a politically incorrect statement in a postmodern culture, where the highest value is freedom, but it seems to me it's quite true. If you give your children total freedom, they will not survive. They will die. If a society tries to live in total freedom, without any form of marriage, family, traffic laws, regulations for what medications are sold, and so on, we won't survive very long. But if there is no freedom, then there is paralysis. That's not a good way to live, either. So freedom is essential for life, but it must be in a complementary relationship with form.

What we tend to do is swing like a pendulum between form and freedom in various sizes of swings. We have historical swings that take centuries, and we have societal swings that can be more rapid, and we have personal swings that can happen several times an hour. I may crave the form, and the security of the form, and then I may move over to the freedom—and often I can't find a good balance between the two. There's always a tension, a struggle, an imbalance. There's always an overemphasis, an incompleteness, a lack of focus in the relationship between form and freedom. There's too much of one or too much of the other. I might have excessive form in my academic life, and excessive freedom in my sexual life, or my friendship life, or my social life. It's difficult to get the whole picture stabilized *and* dynamic. If it's only stable and not dynamic, it's dead, and if it's only dynamic and not stable, it's chaos. How do we get the picture right with dynamic stability? Getting back to your question, a good authority will describe reality in a way that strikes the right balance between freedom *and* form. A bad authority, or a distorted or misused authority, will end up being too extreme one way or the other—allowing too much freedom with no proper form, or too much form and regulation with no proper freedom.

5. What if I don't like the authority of a particular institution? What if it doesn't seem rational? What if, in the case of traffic lights, it's arguably more rational to make green mean stop and red mean go?

It may indeed seem more rational to some people. But knowledge is more than rational. It involves love, humility, submission, cooperation and service. All of these things occur among God, within the relationships of the Trinity. If we are made in God's image, then those elements should be a part of our way of living. To be able to submit is a powerful and humanizing thing—a reality which our contemporary Western culture doesn't know.

Our culture overemphasizes the individual. It overemphasizes personal power and personal achievement. But if we have no capacity for submission, then we'll have problems. We'll lack humility, and service, and cooperation. Although I may agree that it seems more rational for green to mean stop and red to mean go in a traffic light, I also need to balance my rational preference with the authority of tradition, and to submit to that tradition.

The same is true in many other matters in life: sometimes I need to submit.

The first book of Peter tells us that we should submit for the sake of God, not because our government or rulers are perfect, but because God is perfect and He has asked us to do so. Peter also says you should submit to your master (or 'employer' in modern terms). Most of the English translations say that we should submit even if the master is 'harsh', but the actual correct word is *skolios*, which means 'twisted' and even 'crooked'. It means that you should submit to the authority of your master even if he's a dubious character, because the authority is given by God and the master's character is incidental. Of course there is room for other considerations, but the point is, it's stated quite strongly, and so we need to work with that reality.

6. *How do we know that we can trust God?*

We can trust God because He loves us. But how do we know He loves us? That's complicated. We may be taught that it's true, but there is no formula to demonstrate it. The only way to know God is as a living and personal reality. Entering into that reality can be unsettling, because we don't know what to expect.

It's as if you're starving, and you've been offered a bowl of soup, but at the last moment before putting the spoon to your lips, you wonder, 'Is this soup healthy or poisoned?' That's a reasonable question, and there are various ways of finding out the answer. You can interview the cook and see if he's a homicidal maniac. You can wait for others to eat the soup and watch to see if anyone falls over. If you're very bright, you may decide to chemically analyze the soup—although even a chemical analysis may not give you a clear answer, because the soup may react differently in your metabolism, or its properties may change in the cooling process. There are all sorts of variables, but none of them will be sufficient to give you the answer. The only way to really know if the soup is good for you is to eat it. That's living by faith. We eat by faith or we starve to death. Knowledge and reasoning can be helpful, and can inform faith, but they will only take us so far. Faith is necessary.

The Bible tells us *taste and see that the Lord is good*. Normally when we taste we don't see, and when we see we don't taste. God is combining our senses in a holistic way in this statement. Knowing that we can trust God cannot be reduced to one sense. It cannot be reduced to thinking, tasting, seeing, or feeling, but needs to combine all of these and more. On top of all of this, we need to add faith, in order to complete our knowledge that God is trustworthy. We come to God with our whole being.

7. *Does the Holy Spirit help us to know through our feelings?*

Yes, but sometimes what we feel in our hearts can *seem* like the Holy Spirit, when it actually isn't—and in these situations our feelings can contradict the Bible. In my work as a pastor, a woman once came to me and said, 'The Holy Spirit has told me to leave my husband and serve the Lord as a missionary.' I explored the woman's feelings and her situation, which of course wasn't enough. We also explored what the Bible says about the marital relationship, and it was only because of the Bible that I was able to tell her that it wasn't the Holy Spirit guiding her. Although our personal experience is important, there will be situations when, as we put our experience together with what the Bible says, it turns out that our experience is misleading.

8. *Can people misinterpret their own experiences by misreading the Bible?*

That does happen sometimes. For example, people may believe that they love God, when they actually don't, because they have failed to understand what the Bible says about love. The Bible is clear that there's only one way to know that we love God, and that is that we love other people. In other words, we have two different kinds of experiences—the experience of loving God, and the experience of loving other people—and these two experiences must go together. Another way of saying this is that the experience of loving God must be incarnational as well as transcendental. If we have the emotion of loving God, it might be only transcendental; it might be only an idea or feeling that we assume to be connected to the supernatural, but which has no physical practical evidence. The true test of whether our love for God is an actual spiritual experience is whether we love other people. This incarnational experience validates our transcendental experience of loving God; these two experiences happen together in a complementary relationship.

We see a similar dynamic when it comes to faith and works. The apostle James tells us, 'Show me your faith without deeds, and I will show you my faith by my deeds...faith without deeds is dead.' The relationship between faith and works is complementary. We know that we have one when we have the other; if we don't have both, then we don't really have either. People who read the Bible sometimes don't grasp this essential point, and may believe that they have faith based only on a feeling, or based only on activities.

9. Would it be fair to say that you have mixed feelings about postmodernism?

I certainly do. I am grateful for postmodernism because it has restored subjectivity to truth. I am unhappy with postmodernism because it has eliminated objectivity from truth.

10. *Can 'well and story' be applied to experience, rationality, and institution?*

Yes. On the well side of the **I** corner, we may experience our church, or nation, or ethnic associations, or other communities, in terms of our identity, security, and motivation. On the story side of the **I** corner, we may see the whole picture of an institution or of a community, including its history, and where we might fit into that picture. So, on the well side, we may experience pride and encouragement as part of our ethnicity; whereas on the story side, we may see ourselves in the context of the overall community, and understand our role and contributions within this overall frame.

The **E** corner can also be seen in both well and story terms. On the well side, we may experience excitement, or joy, or peace, through experiences such as singing songs, or walking in nature, or skiing. On the story side, we may see our experiences within the overall frame of our lives over time, and understand these experiences in relation to one another. The story side of the **E** corner may overlap somewhat with the **I** corner.

The **R** corner can similarly be understood in well and story terms. On the well side, we may experience curiosity, excitement, and satisfaction, when we explore and learn new things based on reason. Scientists and engineers can probably relate to such experiences. On the story side, we may see how the things we have learned or discovered are related to other areas of knowledge and the historical progression of science. For instance, if I am an aviation engineer and have invented a new type of aircraft, then I may see how this aircraft emerged from earlier models, and how it fits within the progress of aviation history.

11. *How did you arrive at your four epistemological corners? What persuaded you that these corners are a full frame of knowledge?*

The four corners themselves are behind my epistemology. As I've gone through life, I have tried to be rational, and I have seen how reason can help us understand the world. I have lived in various traditions, such as being part of a nation or family, and so I see that such traditions are an important part of understanding reality. I have had personal experiences of great strength, and it seems that they too need to be integrated into knowledge. My life has also been informed by revelation, and that also needs a place. I am always and constantly struggling to integrate these four corners. It never works perfectly. I have to trust God, especially when I can't fully figure it out for myself—which is always. In fact, if I *could* figure it all out for myself, I would not need God, and I would become a humanistic atheist. This is actually what happened to Eve in the Garden of Eden in her encounter with the serpent and the fruit of the knowledge of good and evil. The serpent said to Eve that she would become like God if she ate the fruit and came to know for herself. This is the situation for all of us; we're all eating the fruit, we're all claiming knowledge that makes us independent of God.

12. *Sometimes scientists and pastors disagree on things like the age of the Earth, because they're coming from different corners. What suggestions would you have to encourage a better dialogue in situations like this?*

I would suggest a certain amount of humility. The corners need to be kept together, and seen in complementary relationships. The Bible should not be read in isolation; it was not written for the angels, but for human beings who live in space-time and history, which includes the rational progression of scientific investigation. We have to be careful and not expect the various corners to speak each other's language. The rationality corner is going to be committed to speaking as objectively as possible; but the Bible, being a personal communication, includes subjectivity. For instance, the parables of Jesus are true, and their truth is not confined to objective fact. They are not objectively accurate, but they are true.

13. *Your statement 'not objectively accurate' brings to mind the distinction between 'accurate' and 'non-accurate' truth that you made in your book, 3 THEORIES OF EVERYTHING. This distinction is shown in the 'well and story' columns of the present volume. Can you elaborate on this?*

Allow me to give you an example that I often share with people. If you want to build a true bridge, then you need to approach the project objectively. You need to make exact mathematical calculations. If you do so, then you will be able to build an objectively accurate bridge.

On the other hand, you cannot fall in love accurately. The experience is subjective, with chaotic and unpredictable emotions. You cannot plan the process of falling in love. However, you would not say that falling in love is not true because it is subjective. It is very true—just ask anybody who has fallen in love—but true in a non-accurate way. The objectivity of the bridge is the same for everybody, but the subjectivity of falling in love is unique and exclusive. A more complete experience of truth might be falling in love on a bridge.

14. *Are there only four corners? Are there any more?*

There could be more sources, but I think those four cover most of life. While giving lectures on epistemology, a few people have suggested additional corners, but after some consideration it always turned out that the new corners could be subsumed under the four existing corners.

15. *What you teach about the objective aspect of truth implies definitions of some things. People are often uncomfortable with definitions. Why is that?*

Sometimes people, especially postmodern people, are afraid of definitions, because they fear that definitions will paralyze them. People think of definitions as a point that doesn't move. But a definition is not a point, it's a circle, and in a circle there are infinite points. If I ask Silvio to bring me a cup of tea and he comes back with it, it might be mint tea in a mug, black tea in a cup and saucer, tea with lemon, tea with milk, tea with honey, plant tea, Earl Grey tea, or jasmine tea. There are an infinite number of things that it could be, but it will not be a hammer, because hammer is outside the circle of 'cup of tea'. So is *banana*. So is *chair*. Definition is essential for my life, because if I don't have the definition, I will have to drink a hammer and I will die. In other words, it's life and death to have definitions. Definitions have an authority over meaning, and we need that authority. It isn't a matter of how we feel about it. If someone makes tea for you and puts poison in it, whether you die or not is not a question of whether you have *given* authority to the poison to kill you. The poison has authority whether you give it or not.

Where does authority come from? The Bible tells us that 'All authority comes from God.' That's either true or it's not true. If it is true, then we need to remain and work within that understanding. It doesn't mean that authority is properly used by people, and it doesn't mean we will always like it. It only means it comes from God, because there is authority in and among God. Therefore, we cannot live without authority. We have to have things outside of us that describe reality for us. We can't invent reality for ourselves. Postmodern people move strongly in that direction, of inventing reality for themselves, but I don't think they are really able to do it. I think we all live in a reality that is independent of our attitude.

16. *Some branches of the Protestant church have become very liberal and very critical towards the Bible. Can you comment on this trend?*

This trend is a result of the Enlightenment and scientism becoming the salt and light of the church, by demanding that the Bible's truth be only objective. Many Christians have absorbed this rationalistic expectation. When the Bible doesn't conform to this expectation, liberal Christians can become insecure and abandon the truth of the Bible. On the other hand, fundamentalist Christians can be forced into a corner and try to make the Bible speak only objectively.

17. *How much clarity should we expect when reading the Bible?*

We should expect a great deal of clarity. However, if you demand perfect clarity from your Bible, then the **R** corner is probably dictating how you read it. You are probably interpreting it through very rationalistic glasses. An extreme example of this tendency would be somebody doing research to determine the identity of the mother of the prodigal son. Another example would be trying to identify the precise correspondence of all the images in the parables, and to distill from the parables specific instructions and prescriptions for life. A better way to approach the parables is as windows that Jesus opened, through which we all see reality from different points of view. As I suggested earlier, the parables are an example of non-accurate truth. A further example of non-accurate truth would be the passage in John, chapter 6: 'Whoever eats my flesh and drinks my blood remains in me, and I in them.' This passage is true, but does not lend itself to an 'accurate' scientific reading.

18. *Some people who want to be strong in their Christian faith may stick to the* **B** *corner and avoid the other three corners, fearing the other three corners might cause uncertainty in their faith.*
Any thoughts about this?

I think Christians should consider the possibility that faith in the Bible is strengthened by contextualizing it with the other three corners. We can't go and live inside the Bible; the Bible helps us to live in the world. We don't need to be afraid of any of the corners, although they all have their dangers. None of the corners is safe. The devil tried to distort even Jesus' reading of the Bible (as we see in Luke 4: 9-11)—so not even the Bible corner is completely safe. We shouldn't get too comfortable and fall asleep in any of the corners.

19. *Is it possible for the* **R** *corner to support the* **B** *corner?*

Yes. The **R** corner is the basis for historical and archeological research. During the eighteenth century, many scholars believed that writing had not yet been invented during the time of Moses, meaning that the early books of the Bible must not have been written at the time they are claimed to have been written. However, during the nineteenth century archeologists discovered the Code of Hammurabi, which was written around 1700 B.C. The discovery that people were already writing before Moses gave strength to the view that the early books of the Bible could have been written around the time of the events described in these books.

20. *Christians often want to submit to the Bible. Should we also submit to the other three corners?*

The authorities of all the four corners need to be contextualized with each other, in a complementary rather than a competitive way. We shouldn't submit to any of the corners in isolation, because that would be a form of idolatry. It's taking only a part of reality and absolutizing it. We may find ourselves worshipping the Bible, or experience, or tradition, or rationality, and end up with distortions of our understanding of reality. Remember that each corner is essential.

21. *Some people might argue that we can do fine with just the* **E**, **I**, *and* **R** *corners, leaving out the* **B** *corner. Are there any risks in doing this?*

There are various risks. One is that, if there is a supernatural reality, then only using the **E**, **I**, and **R** corners, without the **B** corner, would leave you open to an awareness of the supernatural, without any guide. Many people say 'I am spiritual but not religious', meaning that they're aware of the supernatural, but they don't have any way to integrate it into the **E**, **I**, and **R** corners. It makes their spirituality highly subjective and unstable. Without the Bible, it's difficult to have any objective aspects to spirituality.

Another risk is that with only the **E**, **I**, and **R** corners, people are working within a humanistic relativism. People need absolutes if they are made in the image of God, who *is* absolute. In a postmodern culture, people are wary of absolutes, and like to think that there aren't any. At conferences where I've lectured, the organizers have made T-shirts that read, 'Are all absolutes absurd?' This question eats itself by the tail, because if all absolutes are absolutely absurd, then so is this one. The only escape from absurdity is to have absolutes, which the **B** corner gives us.

22. *Is there no way to establish an absolute from the objective nature of the* **R** *corner?*

One could arrive at an absolute, but it would be mechanical and impersonal. We humans experience a life that includes the subjective and the personal, so we would not fit or belong in a totally rational or objective absolute.

23. *Muslims and Hindus might take the Bible out of the* **B** *corner and insert some other special revelation or spiritual text, such as the Koran or Vedas.*
How can we know if that version of epistemology is more or less valid than one in which the Bible is in the Revelation corner?

We need to examine the suggested revelatory texts, and see if they fit history and science, and life as we live it. We need to be careful not to approach these texts religiously, by worshipping them or making assumptions that they're true, but by asking questions about them. We should examine the Revelation text (or **B** corner) to see if it complements the other three corners, or if it contradicts them. In my view, the Bible belongs with the other three corners better than any other revelatory text.

24. *Your epistemological framework implicitly recognizes the role of science, which relies heavily on reason. Does art also inform our epistemology?*

Art, or creativity, functions largely in the **E** corner. Art helps us to experience reality and to organize experience in a variety of ways. We should include in art literature, drama, poetry, dance, cooking, conversation, music, sculpting, interior decorating, clothes design, architecture, and of course painting. Good artists want to help people know reality more fully. A principal contribution of artists to epistemology is to show in some way that one thing is like another. The artist says, 'This is like that' and everyone else says, 'Oh, so it is! I never saw that before.' Art can be true or false or helpful or unhelpful, and therefore must always be tested to see if it relates in a complementary manner with the other three corners.

25. *You mentioned that authority functions best when there is trust. Can you say more about trust, and other elements that are important in relationships of authority?*

Relationships of authority do need trust in order to function at their best. When there is no trust, the stance of the person under authority will be one of avoidance, subversion, or rebellion toward the person or institution that has authority. Faithfulness and consistency are also important in authority, as well as respect. For instance, the person who has authority must respect the person who is under authority. Respecting means recognizing that the person under authority has the same value as the person with authority, even though he or she has a different role.

On that note, we also need to have a clear awareness of our role and place in a relationship of authority. As I mentioned earlier, humility is realism. It isn't a matter of what we want or feel like, nor a policy of always being a doormat. It is a matter of being honestly aware of the real situation and condition in which we are.

Sometimes we need the humility to accept that we are *under* authority. Sometimes we need the humility to accept that we *have* authority. Both can be difficult. If we don't accept these realities, we have misunderstanding, confusion, and possibly conflict. Although authority is essential for life, it can often be destructive so we need to be wise and careful about it.

26. *You said that gravity has authority. But if authority is the 'power to describe reality,' in what sense does gravity 'describe' reality? Gravity doesn't talk.*

Talking isn't the only way to communicate or demonstrate something. Gravity 'tells' us that if we jump off a tall building we will be hurt. It's important to listen to this message and take it seriously. 'Describe' means to scribe a line or circle around something and make it defined and distinct from other parts of reality. Gravity draws a line around walking, for instance, and puts it on the ground instead of on the ceiling or in the air.

27. *Has anybody else devised a four-corner epistemological model like yours?*

Yes, John Wesley developed what is called the 'Wesleyan Quadrilateral', which involves four sources of authority for theological reflection. Wesley's four sources, like mine, are Scripture, tradition, experience, and reason. However, the purpose of his Quadrilateral method is theological reflection, whereas my purpose is epistemology. I discovered Wesley's work after I had finished working mine out and was pleased to be in his company.

28. *You often talk about 'reality'. What do you mean by 'reality'?*

Reality is who God is, what He does, and what He wants. That means that evil is unreal, and sin is unreal. God made us to be real, and when we choose to live in unreality, He gets very upset.

When I say 'real', I mean total, comprehensive, absolute Reality, and not some aspect or experience of reality. The same would apply to 'truth'. Truth with a capital T is basically the same as Reality. Truth must include love, because love is part of who God is, what He does, and what He wants.

29. *Before the Bible came into being, could anybody have had a complete epistemology? Similarly, today there may be places and cultures in the world where people have not yet been exposed to the Bible. Is it possible for such people to experience a complete epistemology?*

No one experiences a complete epistemology except God as a Trinity. However, it would certainly be possible for the people in your question to have an epistemology that is adequate for salvation. The first corner, as I've noted earlier, is actually 'Revelation' as well as 'Bible'. That is, God gives us revelation not only through the Bible, but through the creation as a whole, the uniqueness of human beings, and direct revelation. The working of the Holy Spirit is not limited to the Bible; He reveals truth to people through dreams, observations of nature and other ways. God has put eternity in the hearts of all people. The question is how we respond to Him. A 'saving' epistemology must also include faith, whether a person has a Bible in his hand or not.

30. *You mentioned that 'Revelation means information that comes from the supernatural into the natural world.' Can you say a little more about the differences between the supernatural and natural world?*

The natural world, which is created, includes Earth and the physical universe, and is the subject of scientific investigation. The supernatural world, which is also created, includes angels and demons. There is also the supernatural world which is *uncreated*; this refers to God himself, who was not created but has always existed. The supernatural world (both created and uncreated) cannot be fully accessed scientifically, because it exists and functions partly in dimensions that are unavailable to physical investigation.

31. *People say that 'Seeing is believing'. What do you think about that?*

I think it is true. Seeing is believing—but also believing is seeing. For example, because we believe that someone loves us or is trustworthy, we see them differently. We don't only believe because we see; believing changes the *way* we see. When belief changes how we see, it doesn't necessarily make us see more truly, or less truly. Belief needs to be tested by what we see. Seeing and believing belong together. They should work together in a complementary relationship for a full epistemology.

32. *The four corners, and well and story, inform our understanding of reality as a whole. But how do people apply them to their everyday lives? In what areas of ordinary, everyday life can you see an application of the four corners, or the well and story?*

The corners and columns keep us from being unbalanced in our thinking and expectations of life. For example, in the case of marriage, using the corners, and well and story, can help people realize that marriage is not more 'male' or more 'female'. Another example would involve reading texts. We know the meaning of a text in various ways—for instance, by what it says and how I respond to it. Using the corners and columns helps us to keep those ways of knowing in complementarity.

A third example would involve raising children. In this case, the corners and columns help us to keep children within the objective aspect of reality, rather than in a complete fantasy reality; at the same time, it allows them their subjective experience of reality.

33. Can we know if someone is saved?

Salvation means changing from a self-centered, dead condition, to an other-centered living condition by the power of Jesus. Salvation is a fact that has an effect. The Bible speaks of salvation and the assurance of salvation, which are not exactly the same thing. If someone is religious, and has had religious experiences, and does not grow in the fruits of the Spirit (love, joy, peace, patience, kindness, goodness, faithfulness, gentleness, and self-control) there is no evidence or assurance that the person actually belongs to God and has new life in Christ. In such a situation there are two possibilities; either the person was never saved, and there is no new life (this is probably the safest assumption), or the person is saved and having a really rough time. Human beings are not the Holy Spirit, so our epistemology is limited.

Some things only God knows for sure.

Comprehensive Spirituality

Table of Contents

Introduction

Creativity

Rationality

Morality

Emotions

Language

Relationships

The Body

The Supernatural

Comprehensive Spirituality

32 Questions

What is spiritual?

Once, at an Evangelical leadership conference in Poland, I asked people to tell me what they mean when they say "spiritual". Several responses came in rapidly:

Supernatural

Invisible

Something Inside Me

Not Physical

Transcendent

I told people that I found these answers very interesting, as they had just rejected the Incarnation and Resurrection of Christ as unspiritual. The Bible is emphatic that these events were physical. Without Christmas and Easter, Christianity is not what the Bible says it is.

The purpose of this book is to explore and clarify what spiritual means—a subject of much confusion. An understanding of spiritual as supernatural is quite common among both religious and non-religious people. As an equation, this understanding can be expressed as:

spiritual = supernatural

I don't agree with this equation, and would put a line through the equal sign, like this:

spiritual ≠ supernatural

As just mentioned, two central events of Christianity are the

Incarnation and Resurrection of Jesus Christ. When the Bible talks about these events, it emphasizes that they are physical, visible, touchable, and historical.

Perhaps a better equation for understanding spirituality, and the one that will be explored in this book, is the following:

spiritual = totally real

If spiritual equals totally real, then it is important to have some understanding of what reality is. Intelligent and alert students ask about this. Reality is who God is, what He does, and what He wants. This includes you, of course, because God wants you to exist and He made you. It includes the whole natural creation as God intends it to be. It includes the supernatural dimensions, forces, and creatures.

Distortions of who God is, what He does, and what He wants, are not real. They are not permanent but temporary. Eternity is permanent; time is temporary. Time is not evil, but it will end. Sickness, suffering and death, as well as pride, envy and hatred are not eternally real; they too will end. An exception is the suffering of Christ, which happened both in eternity as well as time, and therefore is real.

Within time, we suffer from sickness and death and other things, but they are not part of who God is, what He does, and what He wants. What is not real causes suffering. A paranoid person suffers terribly from delusions that are not real. The suffering does not make the delusions real. The unreal distortions that we experience are things that God wants to save us from and eliminate.

Sin is inventing unreality, and trying to live in it. The reality of God includes, as a major ingredient, humility. If I live in pride and being self-centered, then that is unreal, and I cannot live in that false, invented reality, because there is nothing to sustain it. I have to live in God's reality, of who He is, what He does, and what He wants. If I go outside of that, I will die. It's like the bird choosing not to migrate. It will die. That is why the Bible says *the wages of sin is death*.

Sin is not any particular activity, although particular activities participate in sin. Sin is basically going outside the parameters of reality, rebelling against the very rich reality in which we can have infinitely creative and beautiful lives, and inventing our own reality. That is what sin is, and it happens in big ways and in little ways, in our thoughts and in our speech, and in our actions.

Human beings throughout history have had a natural tendency to worship their imagination, and the imaginations of each other, and to consider them to be real—and sometimes more real than the actual reality. When we do that, it's not possible to live as an individual, as a community, or as a society, because there is no foundation to sustain or support that invented reality.

The way forward is to go back to the Bible, not in a religious sense of memorizing and reciting prescribed texts, or having certain emotional reactions to it, or looking inside ourselves to interpret it, but to read the text and ask, *What is the reality that the Bible describes in basic terms?*

Once we start to see the parameters of that reality, we can start to try and live in that reality, and to invite other people to live in it. For people, who are all sinners, accepting this invitation can produce a great transformation, because it involves going from a largely false reality and false identity to a true one. This change is described in the Bible as being *born again*. To be born again means being remade by the power of the sacrifice of Jesus Christ, and to live in the actual and true reality forever.

The creation is real, but the distortions of the creation that have come through sin are not real. Sin is any distortion, rebellion, departure or addition to reality. God is other-centered and He made people in His image to be other-centered. When we are self-centered and egotistical, that is unreal, and we have suffered terribly from that distortion.

To be spiritual is to be real as we should be, according to God's character and intention. To be spiritual means to belong to God and to fit into His reality. To be unspiritual is to shrink, expand, or distort God's reality. In 1 Corinthians 13, Paul writes about love. Here is another equation:

God is love

Paul tells us that no matter what we do or achieve or make, if we don't have love, we are like a gong in the wind—the sound dissipates and is gone. It is unreal. In the Old Testament, in the Psalms, we read that the person who bases his life on unreality will disappear like a dream upon waking.

Let's consider human spirituality as a series of triangles.

The First Triangle:
Creativity

The background of the first triangle is God. If we want to know what "spiritual" means in the biblical understanding of it, we need to begin with the Bible, which says "God is Spirit". This statement is the same as the statement "God is love", "God is light", or "God is truth". It means that everything about God is spirit, that there is no part of God that is not spirit or spiritual. So, in order to understand what spiritual means, we need to find out from the Bible who God is and what He is like, and then we will begin to get an understanding of what spiritual means in the biblical sense.

The first thing we learn about God in Genesis is that He creates and He speaks. He creates in an original sense of calling something into being that was not there before, such as time, space, and matter. God created the building blocks or foundation of the world, and He created the particular things in it; land, sea, plants, animals, as well as relationships of increasing complexity as the days of creation unfold. Then He said, *Let us create man (people) in Our image.* In creating people in His image, He therefore created them to be creative, because He is creative. If God had not done so, people would not be in His image, and would be incomplete.

The creativity of people is not an original creativity that calls time, space and matter into being, but rather continues the process of God's creativity. That process, according to the Genesis account, is the dividing of reality into parts to create relationships and dynamism. Reality was not meant to be static, undifferentiated matter, but seas and land, animals and plants, with contrasts, relationships, and energetic change. Reality is divided into parts, not for the purpose of exclusion or creating competition, but to make complementary relationships. When God made people, He made them to continue that process in a way that the other parts of creation do not.

People were placed on Earth, initially in the Garden, in order to tend and increase the complexity of the relationships that God had already made. One of the first things we see is that God had Adam name the animals. He divided the animals into a taxonomy, or categories, to make relationships between the animals. When he named them, applying labels to them, that's what they were. Naming them changed the reality. Naming them changed the relationships. The act of naming is a powerful function. A great art critic once wrote that the artist says *This is like that*, and everyone else says *It is! I never noticed that before!*

It is the function of the artist to help people see relationships, and similarly, it was the function of Adam to perceive, describe, and organize the relationships in the creation. The other animals did not have this job. It was only the human beings. Showing relationships through words, image, music, dance, clothing design, architecture, and so on, is not optional for the human being. Without artistic creativity, humans are not in the image of God or spiritual, because God is creative and shows relationships. It is essential to practice this kind of creativity in order to be spiritual.

Creativity can be dangerous. It can go wrong, and be wrongly used for pride, ego, conflict, domination, and evil, but it cannot safely be eliminated. We cannot make ourselves pure and spiritual by becoming uncreative. We need to accept that God has made us to be creative, and we must not refuse to be creative.

Creativity is not restricted to painting and music and other activities we might think of as "artistic". In the most basic sense, creativity involves identifying and organizing relationships, and making new relationships. For instance, wheat naturally grows along the side of streams mixed with other plants. The human being, being creative, says, *Wheat, you will grow in this field, alone.* That is not natural. That is artificial. The human being is called to be artificial. That is what art means. In other words, there's a division between art and nature. If something is natural, it's what God does, and it's right, true, and beautiful, but it isn't art. Art is artificial. It's made by the arm of man. A wheat field is not made by God, it is made by the human being, with imagination, research, experimentation, and physical strength. As a result, there is civilization; people can be stabilized, and don't need to be hunters and gatherers. But it's also art, in that it creates and organizes relationships within what God has made. Cooking, hospitality, interior decorating, conversation, child-rearing, education—all of these, like wheat fields, are creative, because they involve recognizing and organizing relationships.

Creativity is one of the things that makes human beings unique. It is part of God's perfect design and plan. If we say, *No, creativity is too complex and dangerous, and we are going to make our lives pure by eliminating creativity,* then we are disobedient and rebellious. An example of this disobedience would be a person with a talent for writing, who chooses to restrain himself from writing out of fear it is prideful or too powerful and might manipulate people—as if, by living a smaller and narrower life, he can keep his life clean and pure. Jesus said *I have come that you would have life, and have it more abundantly.* He didn't say *I have come that you would have life and have it tidily.* Life is a mess, and Jesus knows that. It's abundant and complex. We don't walk by control and sight, we walk by faith. In situations that are too complex for us to comprehend or control, we need to trust God to keep us safe. We have a natural tendency to reduce and control life, whereas the spiritual tendency is to obey God and to accept the complexity and the responsibility of creativity.

However, there is another and opposite danger. We may try to become God through our creativity. Keeping with the example of writing, the writer may create a fictional world which promotes concepts of human life, relationships, and values in order to replace what God has made. We see this tendency in many movies as well. A quite different example would involve agriculture. We have the power and the mandate to reshape plant life artificially, and to grow things in ways that they would not naturally grow. But this power can be misused to deforest a mountain range, or to cause erosion resulting in dustbowls; in this way, we irresponsibly and stupidly turn nature into our enemy by trying to control it.

The power that God has given us to be creative is not safe. We have to be careful and look as widely and deeply as we can into a situation, in order to be creative in a right way, within the posture of a creature rather than the posture of God. We need to function in a *creaturely* way. We create in the face of God, who has shown us some basic patterns, and we shouldn't replace those basic patterns with our own imaginations. We need to function within those patterns. But it's very complicated; I don't think we can see a way to draw a line, and to say "we figured it out, now we know"—because we don't know. Things change, and we always have to stay awake. We need to think, and talk and pray for wisdom, and that God will restrain us.

It is a natural tendency to want to draw a line to protect us, but it won't work. We will never find the right line, the exact boundary where we can say *this kind of creativity is safe,* and this kind of creativity is unsafe, because God has not designed us to live by law and fact only, but by faith, grace, and relationships, which are dynamic. Lines are static. It's not how God has created us to be.

God is not static. God is both unchanging and changing. We cannot comprehend the nature of God because we are creatures. In order to understand God, we would have to get behind Him and look over His shoulder to see the whole picture. But we can't see the whole picture. We have to walk by faith, not by knowledge or comprehension, though we very strongly want to understand and control. We want to simplify things so that life is easier, and so that "we get it". But the Bible shows us that we don't get it. We constantly need God to guide us, protect us, and restrain us. We need God to keep us safe through the impossible complexity of creativity.

The Second Triangle:
Rationality

The second triangle is rationality. Rational means perceiving reality in relationships, or ratios. It means perceiving that parts of reality are bigger or smaller, faster or slower, brighter or duller, harder or softer. It means seeing a variety of qualities, such as size, intensity, shape, function, and so on, and to see how these different parts of reality relate to each other. The creation account in Genesis shows us specifically, and in detail, that God is rational. The whole process day by day, is creating and observing relationships, and calling them "good". The relationship of the land to the sea—it is *good*. The relationships among plants and animals and water creatures—they are *good*. The creative process is one of creating relationships of greater and greater detail, and rationality means seeing and understanding these relationships.

When God created creatures in His own image, they were rational. They were not rational as creators of the universe, but as unique creatures, different from the other parts of the creation. The non-human creatures do not perceive the creation rationally in the same way that people do. People do it very similarly to the way God does it.

Rationality and creativity overlap in some ways, but rationality is more a process of identifying and seeing with greater clarity what is already there; to be creative is to do something with those relationships, especially by making new relationships. Rationality is observing plants grow, and coming to an understanding of how they grow, whereas creativity is altering the way that they grow, for example by isolating plants in certain fields. Rationality gives us information about things, and therefore is essential; but creativity is also essential, because we do things with what we learn.

To be spiritual is to be the way God made us to be, and to be like God. Rationality is an essential part of spirituality, though it isn't problem-free. We can misuse our rationality. We can rationalize things in a legalistic or mechanical way. We can justify unjust behavior by certain forms of reasoning. We can sin in deadly ways with our logic. That makes people want to be safe, and therefore many people believe and practice becoming less rational. They try to live only by faith, only trusting impulses and instincts, or following their heart, and avoiding thinking things through and making rational decisions, because it feels to them more pure and simple to live only by faith. The goodness of that feeling is identified as a godly feeling, a spiritual feeling, whereas actually it is not. It is more like the feeling of a drug trip. It feels good, and so they think it must be true, when in fact other criteria are needed to evaluate goodness or non-goodness.

To evaluate in terms of how *I feel* is humanistic. It's not Christian. It means *I am God.* My feelings, my reactions, tell me what is good and what is evil. I don't trust God to tell me. I don't trust God's word, which is complicated; I trust my simple feelings, and gut-level ways of relating to the world around me. I protect those ways by keeping them simple and refusing to accept the complications of being rational. People sometimes say, *My mind is made up and don't confuse me with the facts. I'm a simple person of faith. I just trust and obey*—whereas they are neither trusting nor obeying, because they are eliminating the rationality that God intended to be part of their spirituality.

Of course our rationality is limited, for several reasons. First, we are creatures rather than the Creator, which means we never see and understand everything—far from it. Second, our rationality is limited by sin, by the distortions of our minds; and third, by being the victims of the sins of other people, whether our parents, ancestors, or those in our culture. Rationality is never perfect, and ideally it functions in complementarity with the other aspects of our spirituality. If we isolate rationality and expect it to give us life, we'll get death.

Rationality can also be distorted by history and culture. History and culture can swing like a pendulum toward different extremes.

Consider objectivity and subjectivity. The Enlightenment and the scientific revolution made a strong swing toward objectivity and the idea that *truth equals fact*. This swing resulted in various benefits in terms of scientific discoveries, discoveries which I'm actually quite thankful for. But it wasn't a whole picture. One of the things I'm thankful to postmodernism for is that it has restored subjectivity to truth, so that truth is not only objective or factual, but also includes individual and personal points of view. The problem with postmodernism is that, in restoring subjectivity to truth, it has to some extent eliminated objectivity. The one extreme is not better than the other, it's just different. What we need is a complementary balance of fullness and wholeness of objectivity and subjectivity.

How do we get to that balance? We get to it through prayer and trust. We get to it through the work of the Holy Spirit in our lives, transforming us and giving us the mind of Christ, rather than the mind of death. In this way, we can make progress in the direction of balance, although that process never finishes. No one can become perfectly balanced until the Lord appears and makes everything new. Until then, we remain in a situation that is imperfect. Sometimes people try to make things perfect, but perfectionism is a deadly disease—and yet, it is quite understandable, because God made us to be perfect. The longing for perfection is put in us by God; but to claim that perfection can exist through our own efforts, or to fear our lives have no meaning and no value because we haven't arrived at perfection, does not come from God.

Rationality cannot properly operate in isolation. Just as it must be balanced in terms of objectivity and subjectivity, it must be balanced with other areas of spirituality. We'll never get the balance right in a fallen world, though we will one day, in a redeemed world—and when it is right, it won't be right in a static, frozen sense, but in an active and dynamic eternity.

The Third Triangle:
Morality

The third triangle is morality. Moral means being aware of what should be and what should not be. God is moral, as the Bible describes Him. He is aware that He should keep His promises, and not to be unfaithful or fickle. That should comes from Himself. No one created God. There is no uncle standing behind Him saying, *Now you be a promise-keeping God!* He is self-begotten. When Moses met God at the burning bush, Moses asked, *Who are you? What is your name?* God said, *I am that I am.* God is self-purposed, the cause of Himself. From our creaturely point of view that's unimaginable. How can there be a causeless cause? As far as we can see, everything that happens is caused by something else. And yet, God is the sole exception. He is the causeless cause. He is the final reality; and He is the beginning of everything.

God is aware of Himself as a causeless cause, and He is aware of His own nature. He isn't a cosmic gas cloud of love. He is a particular God—a creative, relating, speaking, promise-keeping God. There is a definition to God that He has for Himself and which He tells us about—*This is the way I am.* He knows that He *should* be a particular way. He should be a speaking God and *should not* remain silent. He *should* keep His promises, and He should not lie. He is completely consistent with what should be, and never does anything that He should not. He is faithful to Himself, and to His creation.

When God made human beings in His image, He also made them to be aware of should and should not. He gave them a specific example of that by putting the tree of the knowledge of good and evil in the garden, and telling them, *You should not eat from that tree.* The tree was a real tree, though it is also symbolic. The tree represents being independent and knowing good and evil for oneself, rather than receiving the knowledge of good and evil from God. If I choose to know good and evil from within myself, instead of receiving that knowledge from God, it means that I am God. I describe reality. I am the source of knowledge about good and evil. This knowledge comes from myself.

This belief produces death. It is death because it alienates me from my Creator. It also alienates me from other human beings who likewise have a sense of the knowledge of good and evil coming from themselves, although it's different from mine. So who is right? The differences are so great it doesn't work to say everybody is right, because that would mean there is no wrong. Of course some people like to think there is no wrong. But I've never met anyone who doesn't complain. I've never met anyone who hasn't said, *That's not right.*

But the idea that there is no wrong is strong in our world. You hear people say, *Everything is right,* or *Everything is okay.* Or they say, *There is no right or wrong. We are all on a journey. We don't know where we're going, but we don't need to know, and it's not getting there that's the point, the point is the journey itself.* If we really believed that, we could never logically complain about anything. Instead, we find ourselves compelled to complain, because things are wrong, objectively and subjectively. Everybody experiences things being in some way wrong—wrong in the world around them, and wrong in themselves.

The belief that everything is right, and that we are okay as we are, is an especially attractive idea. It reflects our natural tendency to want to be rich in spirit. But this is not what the Bible teaches. In the Sermon on the Mount, in which the King, Jesus, gives the manifesto of the Kingdom, the first point is poverty of spirit. Poverty of spirit means *I know that I need God.* To have richness of spirit is to know that *I am good in myself, and self-sufficient. I have a right to be affirmed. I don't need to be forgiven, I need to be empowered. I need society to give me what it owes me. I am entitled.*

I am okay in myself. Poverty of spirit is to realize I'm not fine, I'm not okay. I need to be forgiven. I need to be changed. I need to be healed. That is the first point of the Kingdom of heaven: If you don't have poverty of spirit, you will never have any relationship to the Kingdom of heaven.

Trusting in the message of Jesus is not purely a matter of faith. If I observe my life honestly, then what I observe is a mess. I see my wretchedness. I experience my alienation from others. The Bible encourages me to see that my life is a mess not because I was *made* a mess, but because I have *chosen* to mess myself up. Sometimes it can be hard to admit these things. Our natural pride can get in the way of seeing ourselves clearly. We can also be made blind by evil forces that want to consume us. The Bible teaches that the devil prowls around like a lion seeking whom he may devour. The devil speaks to people and encourages them with deadly thought forms and processes, empowering them for death. The combination of these two forces, our pride and an evil agency, can prevent us from recognizing the fundamental importance of poverty of spirit. They can prevent us from knowing that we need God.

Although the idea that *I am okay* is popular nowadays, the Bible is clear that people have believed this for all of history. Evil is very powerful, and people both get sucked up into it, and choose it, because it seems attractive. Once they have chosen it, it can become habit-forming; then people build a fortress around what is wrong and call it right. We defend our pride. We defend ourselves by saying, *No, I'm fine, this is the right way to go.* That's a real trap, and people need to be delivered. They need to be broken free of their enslavement to death. All of us are caught in this trap in one way or another, and all of us need to be set free.

Religious people, including Christians, often want very clear moral lines. It's true that some lines are drawn for us by God, and those should be accepted. A difficulty with those lines is that people exaggerate them, or minimalize them, or in some way distort the lines. Basically, the line that God has given us is the line between being self-centered and being other-centered. If we concentrate on ourselves getting and being served, and being affirmed in who we are in isolation, then we're moving in the wrong direction. If we think in terms of others, meaning God and other people, and how we contribute to and serve them, then we're moving in the right direction. So, it's probably better in some ways to think of a *direction* rather than a *line*. A moral line is not wrong, but a line is not enough. For instance, the Bible is clear that adultery is wrong. It's a line and we should not cross it. But when Jesus speaks about adultery, He speaks about adultery of the mind and the will, not just physical sex. He is speaking more in the sense of *what direction are you moving*. So if you refrain from having physical sex with someone that is not your spouse, you can still move in the direction of death through imagination, longing, obsession, and pornography. You can't just look at moral situations narrowly and think, *I haven't crossed the line, so I'm okay.*

God is the same God, with the same moral characteristics, throughout the Bible, both in the Old and New Testaments. That means God is morally consistent. Of course you will encounter people who claim that God is morally *inconsistent,* though they tend to hold this position as a matter of faith. It's also an excuse. If they can believe that God is wrong, then they're free. They can say, *I don't owe anything to God. There is no Creator. I just appeared evolutionarily like a mushroom out of the mold. I can be my own God.* That's a very strong impulse in the fallen world. It's another example of being rich in spirit.

When people approach me about the supposed inconsistency of God, I generally ask them, *What are the examples that you have in mind?* In my experience most people don't have any clear examples. They tend to offer more vague ideas like, *Isn't it true that the God of the Old Testament is legalistic, whereas the God of the*

New Testament is loving? But if you examine the Bible carefully and comprehensively, which most people don't, you find out that this claim of two Gods, one loving and one legalistic, is not true. It's the same God in both the Old and New Testament. So my advice is, if the question of God's consistency has any importance to you, then look into it. Investigate it thoroughly.

Along with carefully examining the Bible in order to understand God's consistency, I encourage people to carefully examine themselves. Sometimes people say, *Why doesn't God do something about evil, if He is all-powerful and all good?* My response to that is, *If God would do something about evil, what would He do about you?* This question can be a useful question. It's one of the most important questions that people wondering about God's moral character can ask themselves. If you are honest with this question, and honest in your investigation of the Bible, you will come up with answers that may surprise you. However, just because the question is useful doesn't mean that people will pay any attention to it. People are often like Teflon to these kinds of questions. In the New Testament, Jesus Himself, God incarnate, asked people questions, and they just slid off them like non-stick surfaces. God Himself was speaking to them face-to-face and it didn't help! Their pride was so strong that they had committed themselves to not considering any possibility other than what they believed. That was two thousand years ago. People are in the same situation now.

Pride can be so powerful and alluring that it can make it hard to see why we need poverty of spirit. When we have poverty of spirit, we accept ourselves as God has made us to be. We also accept God's opinion, which is much more positive than our own opinion—because God's opinion of us is that we are *worth* dying for. That is shocking. That is part of the scandal of the Gospel. God says *I made you, I love you. You are a wonderful creature, and you are lost. You are worth dying for. I want you to be with me so much that I'm going to die in order to have your company.* You can't have a higher opinion than that. You can't get more positive than that. The negative side is that you have to die. You have to die to your ego, your pride, your self-centeredness, your desire to invent yourself.

Dying like this is no easy thing. It can be painful and frightening. The positive is that you get a much greater life. You die to your deadly self, but you live in Christ. The positive far outweighs the negative, although the negative is not negligible. The prospect of dying can be excruciating. It can seem like open-heart surgery without anesthetic. I'm sympathetic to this fear, but as a Christian and a pastor I'm constantly encouraging people: Trust God. Endure the pain. Endure the shock. Die to your deadly self so that you can live in Christ. Choosing life may be hard, but it's shocking that people don't want life. It's shocking, yet common and understandable given all the pressures, temptations, and natural proclivities of human existence.

The Fourth Triangle:
Emotions

According to the Bible's description of God, He has emotions. He desires that people would live and not die. He desires that people would be well. He desires that people would be with Him and enjoy Him, and that He would enjoy them. He is angry when that doesn't happen—when people turn away from Him and destroy themselves or destroy each other.

We don't understand the emotions of God particularly well, but the Bible clearly says that they're there. Therefore, when God made creatures in His image, He made them to be emotional. We see this in the creation account. Adam was functioning as a human, but alone, which God said was *not good*, because the image of God is *them*, not *him* or *her*. Adam was just *him*, not them. Something essential was missing. When God made Eve, Adam was full of emotion and sang a kind of song in parallel Hebrew poetry. He was excited. Emotions were a part of who he was. They were present from the beginning.

We can make two mistakes when it comes to emotions. One is that, as we realize emotions are not stable and not trustworthy, we may try to avoid our emotions and make our spirituality only rational. We may try to simplify things and reduce our emotions. But to do so is wrong and destructive, because God made us to have emotions and to experience them.

The other mistake is to understand spirituality as only emotional. People may try to look for ways to induce emotional experiences, for example through contact with people, or by listening to certain kinds of music, or viewing certain kinds of art, or speaking in particular ways. People identify their private emotions, as well as public emotions they share, as spiritual, and end up discounting rationality or other aspects of spirituality. They feel safe and right with God, because they repeatedly have certain types of emotions they identify as spiritual. This tendency is a serious problem and a reduction of what spiritual means.

Both our emotional and rational sides are essential, but neither is entirely trustworthy. Still, people will tend to emphasize one or the other, and in doing so try to limit or eliminate the other. Rationality and emotions need to work together. Rationality without emotions isn't life. It's a computer. Emotions without rationality is also a problem, a problem of a different kind, though equally distorting.

In favoring emotions, people often gravitate toward certain types of emotion in defining spirituality. Emotions of happiness are often favored over emotions of fear or shame, although the Bible teaches us that fear and shame are part of what we should experience in a fallen world. We don't like those emotions, of course, and so it's the emotions that we prefer, the ones we identify as pleasant and pleasurable, that we tend to identify as spiritual.

I believe there is an emotion which, for lack of a better term, I would call hugeness. Think of what it feels like to be in an electrical storm, amid all the wind, lightning, and thunder. A feeling can arise in this situation which isn't fear, isn't joy, or anything like that, but *hugeness*—and people often identify *that* with spirituality. But I'd actually identify that feeling with the mob-like emotions of radical groups. Honestly, I myself have experienced that emotion in gatherings of thousands of Christians all singing together—a rush of the emotion of hugeness, which I really enjoy. I get exactly the same feeling when I listen to Beethoven, who wasn't particularly religious.

Some people think the feeling of hugeness or similar feelings, when they occur in a church, is the feeling of the Holy Spirit in them. But I doubt that the work of the Holy Spirit in our lives is principally experienced emotionally. I wouldn't eliminate emotion from the work of the Holy Spirit, but I wouldn't put the emphasis on it, because emotions can be counterfeited. Other workings of the Holy Spirit in our lives, like the fruit of the Spirit, are much more difficult to counterfeit. For instance, patience, kindness, goodness, and faithfulness are hard to fake. But emotions can be faked or stirred up fairly easily. You might even become less spiritual as your preferred emotions *increase*. I would put the emphasis on actual changes in our lives and attitudes when considering whether the Holy Spirit is working in us, rather than on the emotions we feel.

Sometimes people don't want to think carefully about their feelings. They may experience their feelings in a vague or fleeting way, and want to keep it that way. Then I would ask, *Would you also like to not know what food is poison and what food is nutritious?*

Some people seek out the experience, or feeling, of *oneness* with everything. They may find this experience through certain drugs, such as psychedelics, through certain forms of meditative practice, and sometimes through monist religions, such as Buddhism or Hinduism. But the experience of oneness is death. What does that mean? Consider that the beginning of reality is the Trinity, which is both one and many, both unified and diversified. When the Bible speaks of evil, it speaks of the devil, Satan, the accuser, who is only unified, with no diversity. There are no relationships within evil. It's like a black hole. Black holes are described as singularities, which is significant. The singularity is death; life as we know it cannot function in a singularity.

Some people claim that experiences of oneness can increase our feelings of peace and our compassion for others. I believe these people are sincere in their claims, but sincerity is not a criterion for truth. The devil is an angel of light, and attractive. The idea of oneness is attractive, but it is death. Of course death, in this sense, gives at least temporary benefit. It feels good. If we didn't enjoy sin, we'd never do it. The power of sin is its attractiveness. To properly assess experiences such as oneness, we always need to back up and remember a vital theological question: What is reality like? That is, what is *God* like? What does the Bible tell us? The Bible is quite clear that God is diverse. Jesus says *The Father and I are one.* There is a unity. But He also says, *I can only teach you what the Father teaches me. I don't know when the end of history will occur, only the Father knows.* So there is a difference between Jesus and the Father. When Jesus prays to the Father, He's not talking to Himself. He's talking to someone else. An extreme emphasis on unity—as in the idea of oneness—will not take diversity seriously at this fundamental level. As a result, it will distort and destroy reality.

If we want to avoid distorting reality in this way, then it would be useful to live within the circumference of reality. That can be difficult, as many people have lost any concept that there is a limit to reality. We have been taught that reality is how we feel about it. The meaning of a text is my response to the text. In dealing with such tendencies, I might ask people, *How are you feeling about gravity today? Do you feel that gravity pulls toward the Earth or pushes away from it—and let me respect how you feel.* Of course it doesn't matter at all how a person feels about gravity. It's a given. God has given us gravity, and although we may feel a variety of ways about it, those feelings don't change the reality. If we follow our feelings, it can be dangerous, especially if we feel very strongly that we can fly. So, it's important to realize the limits of the reality of our feelings. Not that they're not real, and not that we don't have to deal with them, and not that they aren't powerful and a part of who we are. But there is a limit on the power of feelings to create reality, and we need to respect that limit.

Within Eastern worldviews, the word *compassion*—rather than love—is often used in connection with oneness, and rightly so. Love is a face-to-face relationship. Love is exclusion and embrace. I realize you are different, you are other, you are there, and therefore I can embrace you. But if I experience unity with you, I cannot embrace you. I just hug myself. Compassion is an emotion and an activity that supports and draws people into an experience of unity. Love, although it can be an emotion, is primarily a series of choices that encourages the other person to be who they are, as other. That is how the Bible describes reality as it actually is.

When people refer to the *peace* that comes with oneness, it's hard to know what this precisely means, although, beyond a feeling, it often seems to refer to a *lack of conflict*. But that isn't peace in the biblical sense. In the Bible, peace refers to *shalom*, which means *the provision of a platform and a framework in which to have conflicts*. So, the peace of Jacob with God was expressed in wrestling. Jacob wrestled *with* God, not *against* God; and he wrestled for truth and identity. He became Israel—*he who wrestles with God, struggles with God*. Peace is not the elimination of struggle, but a stable context in which we can have struggle, and grow in truth. The elimination of struggle, of conflict, is the elimination of life.

At a global level, an increasing belief in the feeling of oneness can make people more susceptible to control, politically, economically, religiously, and in other ways. It would probably lead to dictatorship.

The Fifth Triangle:
Language

One of the first things we learn about God in the Bible is that He speaks. We learn that His speech creates reality. *Let there be light,* and there was light. *Let there be seas and land,* and there were seas and land. God spoke these things into reality. Then He made people in His image through words, and brought the animals to Adam to see what he would name them. He brought them, not to see if Adam would guess their names, or if he would remember the list of names that God had provided, but to see what he would name them out of his own imagination, out of his own formulation and creativity. Whatever Adam called the animals, that is what they were. As we saw, the animals were changed by being named, by being put in a taxonomy. T.S. Eliot wrote in his *Four Quartets: ...the roses had the look of flowers that are looked at.* In other words, once they are looked at, the roses are different from the flowers that haven't been looked at. Similarly, animals that are named are different from animals that have not been named. The human being has the power of language, the power to shape reality. We do not shape reality in the original sense of God creating reality out of nothing, but in the sense of *reshaping* the reality, of continuing the organizational process of developing relationships through language. So language is essential to human nature.

In order to be spiritual, we cannot eliminate language. It has to be there, but like the other triangles, it's not safe. We can misuse language. We can lie, we can manipulate it, we can use it in the wrong way. But we cannot be spiritual *without* language.

We need to take language seriously, and also need to rejoice in it. If we don't take it seriously, we can't rejoice in it. We need to acknowledge the power of language, and to acknowledge our responsibility in using it carefully. We need to say what we mean and mean what we say. We must not pretend that language is unreal, or that it has no effect. We should not constantly say *whatever* at the end of every sentence, or qualify everything by saying *like,* instead of what it actually is. We must not minimize the reality of language, or the power that it actually has.

When we take language seriously, we rejoice in our capacity to use it for description, for commitment, for relationship, for encouragement and enabling. Language has an enlivening function. Taking it seriously means learning to express ourselves using a variety of words. It means being aware of clichés, proverbs, or cultural phrases and examining those to find out what they actually mean, and whether we really mean those things, or if we hide behind them. Do we speak in a committed way, or do we hide behind groupthink? These are the kinds of issues we need to consider in order to deepen and enrich our use of language.

Clichés are especially problematic. Their meaning can be distant, diffuse, and broad. People rely on them, but they're not a direct, committed communication. Clichés don't promote relationships. They promote a shallow kind of identity. We may identify with other people who use the same clichés, and feel that we have a relationship with them, or belong with them in some way, but that's hardly any relationship at all. But if I speak what I mean to say, even if another person disagrees with me, then that's in fact a closer relationship. We speak to each other about a subject, and we know we see it differently. That's much closer than mouthing the same cliché.

We also see an increasing use of images and icons to express ideas. Images can be effective in some ways, but reductionistic in others. For instance, an emoji will not fully or clearly express an idea, whereas if I formulate a sentence to give to someone, it will be more direct, responsible, and meaningful.

Some people may feel they are not good at language. They may struggle with this aspect of spirituality. We all struggle with one or several aspects of spirituality. That's part of reality. It wouldn't be wise to say, *This part of spirituality is a struggle, so I'm going to eliminate it or despise it, or pretend it has no importance.* That would be a huge mistake. Life is hard. We need to encourage each other in the struggle of life. If someone struggles with language, then we need to support them and help them see that they do have linguistic powers that haven't been developed yet, and help them to become excited about the possibilities. The same could be said for emotions, rationality, and all the other aspects of spirituality. This is what love means. It means to act and speak in ways that encourage the other person in who God wants them to be. God wants us to be rich and powerful in all these different parts of spirituality. Each person tends to be stronger in some parts and weaker in other parts. We have a natural tendency to strengthen what is strong, and to ignore what is weak. But we have a spiritual tendency to strengthen what is weak, without ignoring what is strong.

Unfortunately, people tend to consider what comes most naturally to them as spiritual. That's a profound confusion between the natural and the spiritual. A person who is more naturally rational than emotional will have a tendency to call rationality spiritual, and to consider emotions a kind of voodoo. Instead, we need to encourage each other in our spiritual tendency, which is to have a more equal complementarity of the different aspects of spirituality.

The Sixth Triangle:
Relationships

The Bible tells us that God is three Persons. They are not identical to each other, and in some ways they are opposite. For example, the Father commands and sends, and the Son obeys and goes. There is a dynamic variety of function and point of view in God, in the original reality. The Persons of God speak to each other, and have a hierarchical relationship with each other. Hierarchical relationships may be politically incorrect today, but Jesus was clear about the issue. He said that He could not teach anything He did not receive from the Father. He also said He does not know when history will end—only the Father does.

God objectively exists. The three persons of God each objectively exist. The persons of God seeing each other from their different points of view is subjectivity. The Father exists objectively and does not change. He is faithful to His character. The Son and Holy Spirit see the Father from different points of view, and so, although they are looking at the same objective Person, some of what they see from their subjective points of view is different. The Son sees perfectly, and the Holy Spirit also sees perfectly, so the differences in what they see are perfect.

One of the implications of this for the Christian life is that Christians should not be clones of each other, seeing everything in exactly the same way. The relationship between Christians should not be one of identity but complementarity, which means acknowledging, respecting, and treasuring the differences we have from each other. On the sixth day of creation, God said, *Let Us make man in Our image.* Then He created Adam. The other days, when He created the lands, the sea, the stars, the plants, the animals, He said, *It is good,* and even, *It is very good.* But, as mentioned earlier, when He created Adam He said, *It is not good.* What was not good is that Adam was alone. *It is not good that the man should be alone.* The reason it wasn't good is because God is not alone.

Here is a proverb I made up: *God alone is God, and God is not alone.* And yet, Adam, in the beginning, was alone. There was no other. He could relate to God, which is essential and beautiful, but *within* the creation there was no one for him to relate to. Adam was aware of himself, and aware of his environment, and had an effect on his environment in naming the animals. Most people would think Adam was personal, but he wasn't. To be personal requires relationships with other persons. To be personal is very different from identity—from "self-being". It is self-being in relationship with other self-beings. Adam didn't have that. He only had himself. God brought the animals to Adam to see what he would name them, and perhaps for Adam to discover that there was no parallel relationship for him with the animals.

Animals are different from human beings. So are plants. They function within the parameters of what God made with total faithfulness. For instance, many birds are made to migrate. They migrate every year without fail, often on the same day, or they die. Similarly, if you hike up the Alps and see a flower, you notice that ten meters higher you don't see that flower anymore. If the seeds from that flower drift a few meters too high or too low, they won't germinate, or they germinate and they die, because they, like other plants and animals, have a natural habitat and natural ways of functioning. If they go outside those parameters, they die, they can't exist. But the human being, who is made in God's image, changes the patterns. The human being is the pattern-breaker. The human being tends the garden, the human being begins with what God has made, and makes changes to it. It's like the example I gave about wheat. God made wheat, and then human beings made wheat to grow alone in fields. That's the kind of radical pattern change that the human being makes, and that the other animals (or plants) don't. But that doesn't make them personal. There has to be another self-aware person to relate to in order to be personal.

In a very real sense, one person is not in the image of God. Of course it's commonly thought that each person, each individual, is in the image of God, but the creation account shows that's not true. The Lord's Prayer also shows that's not true. The Lord's Prayer begins with *Our Father, not My Father*. It's not just me and God. Jesus has no concept that I would relate to God totally alone, that He would be my personal God and I would have a private relationship with Him. I have to relate to God in relationship with other people.

So Adam named the animals, and that was a powerful thing because it changed their nature. The act of naming made a difference in the world. But still the situation was not good because Adam was alone. There was no one to relate to in the Creation. So then God made Eve. Eve was similar to Adam in many respects; for instance, she was a pattern breaker like he was, had a subjective point of view, and so on, but she was also different from Adam. She wasn't a clone of Adam. There's a peculiar proverb in America: God made Adam and Eve, not Adam and Steve. Often this proverb is used against the gay community, but its real meaning speaks to something more fundamental. God didn't make human beings to look for sameness and to live within identity, but to live in relationships with differences. In the right relationship of Adam and Eve, there is a third—a child. That is how people are, basically, anywhere you look in history. There is a mother, father, and a baby. So, in a real sense, human beings come in sets of three, which shouldn't be surprising. God is three Persons, and His image is three Persons. People are Trinitarian. When God finished making Adam and Eve, and Adam and Eve were relating to each other, the Bible text says, *God made people in His image, in His image He made them*. So the image of God is not him or her, but them, in relationship.

The idea that people are Trinitarian has been individualized by some Christian teachings, in particular suggesting that each person is a tripartite organization of body, soul, and spirit. I believe this teaching is problematic, because it leaves out some things, like heart and mind. In that way, it's not comprehensive. But the bigger problem is it's all about the *self*, whereas Christianity is all about the *other*. It's about loving your neighbor as yourself, not about loving yourself. It's not about having a private relationship with God, but about having a relationship in a community—of family, friendship, neighborhood, church, business, nation, and other communities. So it seems to me more true to say that the human being does have a tripartite nature, but it isn't mind, body, and spirit; it's mother, father, and child. That is basic spirituality. So spirituality is not a private thing. You cannot really say, *I am spiritual.* You can only say, *We are spiritual.*

Today people want to believe they invent themselves. But the Bible teaches that we are given who we are. The fallen nature and sin of the world distorts what we are given, but fundamentally we are given who we are. When people insist on inventing themselves out of their longing, pain, or imagination, then they take away the possibility they are given anything. As a result, people can become very lonely. They can also put tremendous pressure on themselves, not only to invent themselves, but to sustain that invention. This pressure is especially hard on children and teenagers. I believe this is why we see increasing rates of suicide among youth. They cannot bear the pressure of being their own God. They cannot bear the pressure of creating themselves out of their own imagination.

The Seventh Triangle:
The Body

It is not possible to be spiritual without a physical body. Many people, if not most people, think of spiritual as transcendent and non-physical. But "spiritual" as described in the Bible is a fuller reality. God has created the physical world and He loves it. He has promised to restore it and sustain it forever. God's reality is not divided into spiritual and non-spiritual; it is all spiritual. Spiritual means a full and integrated reality; that which is partial and disconnected is unspiritual.

God's original intention was to have a physical incarnated body. God's original intention for us was also to have a physical body. The idea that "spiritual" does not include the physical is very old, and even the disciples of Jesus were troubled by it. Jesus's victory over death on the Cross resulted in His new spiritual resurrection body. When the disciples saw this body, they saw it through Platonic or Greek eyes. Palestine had been a Greek colony for three hundred years, since Alexander the Great, and the Greeks had control of the educational system. Jewish boys had absorbed Platonic thought, which includes the transcendental notion that "the idea" is more real than *the actual thing*—which the Old Testament doesn't teach. So, when the disciples saw Jesus appear to them in the locked room where they were staying, they thought they saw a ghost or a supernatural being. The first thing Jesus did was to tell them, *No, I am not a ghost, touch me. I am fully real.* He also asked them to give Him something to eat, and He ate it in their presence. In the new spiritual kingdom of God, touching is spiritual and eating is spiritual. The disciples were startled because Jesus did not come to them through the door or the window. He was able to appear to them, to simply materialize, because He was functioning both in the space-time dimensions, and the non-space-time dimensions, of reality. That is why He can teleport, appear and dematerialize. Jesus, in His resurrection body, functions in the whole reality. We function in, and are aware of, only part of the whole. When we become spiritual—fully spiritual one day in a redeemed world—we will be able to function in the whole reality, being totally real. That includes having a physical body.

In the Book of Luke, we read of Jesus meeting two disciples on their way to Emmaus. Emmaus is about four miles from Jerusalem, so it takes about two hours to walk the distance. The disciples were going home. Most paintings and etchings of Jesus meeting these two disciples shows two men. But it wasn't two men, it was Cleopas, who is named in the Biblical text, and Mrs. Cleopas—Mary Cleopas—who was present at the crucifixion. These two disciples are feeling down and disheartened at Jesus's recent death and all that has happened since then. Jesus said to them, *Why are you so sad?* They responded, in effect, *Are you a tourist? Don't you know what has been going on? The whole city is in an uproar. We thought the Messiah had come, but He was killed, although now there are some women who say they've seen Him alive, and we don't know what to do or think.* Jesus replied, *You are so slow of heart!*—and then He opened up the Scriptures and He showed them, from beginning to end on this long walk, why the Messiah must die and rise again to new life.

Then they reached Emmaus and they made Him come in and sit down to supper. In a Jewish home, then and now, at the beginning of the meal, the father picks up bread, and says, *We bless you, oh God, King of the universe, who gives us bread.* Then he breaks the bread and the meal begins. But when they sat down, Jesus grabbed the bread, which must have been a bit shocking. It was as if He was saying, *This is my house, I am the host here. This is my bread and I'm in charge.* Then He said the customary prayer, and He broke the bread and disappeared. At that point, the two disciples didn't say, *Weren't our hearts burning within us when He disappeared?* No. And they didn't say, *Weren't our hearts burning within us when He grabbed the bread?* What they said was,

Weren't our hearts burning within us when He talked with us on the road? So when Jesus was working with their heads, their hearts were burning, which shows us that the difference between the head and the heart is nothing. It all belongs together. Thinking, understanding, and perception are all part of spirituality. Spirituality is not only a transcendental or emotional reality. It's a rational and sensing reality as well.

In John 21: 4-13 we read about Jesus coming to the disciples at the Sea of Galilee. They had been fishing all night by torchlight, and He seems to say, *Hey guys, did you catch anything?* They replied, No, we didn't. He encouraged them to put in the net one more time. They replied that they had been doing it all night, but He insisted, so they did and landed an enormous catch. This was a miracle, but Jesus is the Creator of the universe and called the fish into the net. Then it dawned on the disciples who it was that was talking with them. They came to the shore and saw some surprising things. They found that Jesus had built a fire. He had been working, in other words. He had also baked bread, so He had been creative, and had broiled fish too. So we see that work is spiritual, and creativity is spiritual, because the resurrected glorified Christ did both. Then Jesus said, *Come, and have breakfast,* which shows us that practicing hospitality is also spiritual.

In the post-resurrection appearances above, Jesus is present physically, and emphatically so, walking, speaking, eating, working, which tells us that the physical body is also essential to spirituality. It tells us our physical body will be sustained by God forever. So, when we try to be spiritual, we should not try to neglect, or leave, or transcend the body. We should take the body seriously, not self-centeredly or narcissistically, but in the way God intended. We should thank God for it, and rejoice in it. Our physical body is not something that God is going to throw away.

It is something that He made, and will transform, along with transforming our minds and our hearts, and keep with Him, for us, forever.

The risen Jesus, as described in the Bible, is the final spiritual reality. There is no next step. Nothing else happens. This is it. Jesus is natural and supernatural. He is transcendent and immanent. When we belong to Him, *that* is the direction we are moving. Of course we don't know everything about what it will be like to be fully restored in this way, but we see indications of it in the resurrected Jesus, and we see it at the end of the Bible, in the wedding supper of the Lamb. That supper is not going to be the exchange of nutritious waves of ectoplasm between glowing light spheres. It's going to be broiled fish, and bread, and food of all kinds. People will enjoy it. They might even comment on the flavor. Of course there will be much more to that redeemed existence, because we'll be living in all the dimensions of reality, and we don't fully know what it will be like. What we can say, for certain, is that it will be a larger, richer, and more interesting life than the one we have now. Nothing will be taken away from what we have, except for our tears, weeping, pain, and mortality; but we will still have emotions and perceptions. There will not be any general reduction of life in order to have a spiritual life. Rather, things will be added to the life we already have. We cannot experience the fully redeemed existence now, but we can believe, accept, rejoice, and anticipate what is to come, through faith.

The Eighth Triangle:
The Supernatural

We have considered seven different aspects of spirituality, all of which are essential and work in a complementary relationship, forming a full spirituality. But one thing we have not talked about is the supernatural, which includes angels, demons, realms and powers, and prayer and the work of the Holy Spirit in our lives.

We are always in the presence of the supernatural, not only sometimes. To be spiritual requires the inclusion of the supernatural, and not living only in the created space-time continuum. We need to be in relationship with the *uncreated* reality, which is God. Sometimes I refer to the supernatural as the eighth triangle of spirituality, although I don't often emphasize it, because most Christians (and non-Christians) already know that spirituality involves the supernatural. The problem is, many people think that's all it involves, and that's why I emphasized the other seven triangles—to show that spirituality is more than the supernatural, although it's not less than the supernatural.

Prayer is a relationship with God. Some people want to learn about prayer techniques. Sometimes there can be techniques, but if prayer gets reduced to a technique, it is no longer what God intends it to be. Relationships are not techniques. Relationships are often the very opposite, even somewhat mysterious. The situation between ourselves and God is similar to a marriage. We are the bride of Christ. He is our husband, and we relate to Him in a variety of ways, one of which is prayer. People confuse prayer with meditation, transcendence, or emotional experiences; but fundamentally, prayer involves speech. It involves words. At the end of the prophecy of Hosea, he says, *Take words with you, and return to the Lord.* It may sound a little bit comical, like bring them in a bucket, but remember that the first thing we learn about God is that He speaks. His speech has effect, and He is faithful to His speech. The first thing we learn about people, as well, is they have speech. Adam named the animals, and his speech had effect. Words and speech are essential and basic to God and to God's image, human beings.

We can't overestimate the importance of words. We need to use them carefully. I've heard Christians use expressions like, *It's only words*. My response is, *What else is the Bible? What else in the Bible do we have, besides words?* There is nothing else. It's only words. Words are essential to human conversation and to prayer. When Jesus taught His disciples to pray, He didn't teach them a posture or breathing technique, or a particular mantra. He encouraged them, and us, to talk with God. He gave us his prayer, the Our Father. He wants us to talk to God together, because He said not, *My Father*, but *Our Father*. Words connect us with the supernatural.

Often we hear in church that we should listen for God's voice in our prayers or lives. There is a sense in which this is true, and a sense in which this is misleading. God has already spoken to us through the Bible, and so we can hear God's message to us, communicated through the people who wrote the Bible. It is essential to listen to (read, study, and pray about) this message. But, apart from the Bible, can we ever literally hear God speaking to us?

The Bible describes quite a few people hearing the voice of God in the Old Testament and New Testament. What's interesting to me is that none of them were listening for or expecting to hear God's voice. It was a total surprise to all of them. It was even a shock to some of them. The apostle Paul on the road to Damascus was not listening for the voice of God. It came as a surprise, and knocked him to the ground and blinded him. But God did speak to him. God speaks in His time, and in His way, clearly and specifically to some people, and not other people. But He has spoken richly and generally, through the creation and the

Bible, in the Incarnation of Jesus Christ and the uniqueness of the human being. These express God's Word, and the effect of His Word, and we should give careful attention to them. But to believe that God will speak a personal word to me, apart from the Bible, is a different matter.

Some people still expect it. They listen for God's voice about various concerns, such as whether to *buy a Ford*, or, *give money to the Pakistani mission*, or, *elect this elder and not that one*. It is possible God will speak personally to you in a prayer, but according to the Bible, *listening* for Him to speak doesn't seem to have a big effect on hearing Him. Rather, the Bible tells us that when He speaks, we hear, irrespective of whether we're listening for Him or not.

What does this mean practically? Let's say we are trying to decide whether to buy that car, that Ford we saw at the dealership, although our financial situation is tight. We know that God is a God of big things and of little things, and that everything matters to Him, and so we want to make sure that we use our money wisely. What should we do? Can we pray to God about this for guidance? Of course we can, and should. We could pray for wisdom. We could pray for sensitivity to circumstances to help us make a good decision. However, when we ask God to make the decision for us, very often *He says, No, you decide. You're a human being, not a puppet. I'm not deciding for you.* You decide. But it's still good that you bring the question to God, because we are taught in Philippians, *In everything, by prayer and supplication, bring your requests to God*. It doesn't say just bring the things He might be interested in. It says everything. That includes the Ford. But He's not going to dehumanize us by dictating to us all the details of our lives.

Sometimes miracles can happen in response to prayer. We may be sitting at the kitchen table, and suddenly we get a phone call from our friend in Oklahoma who says, *Hey, I've got this old Ford I don't need any more, do you know anybody who needs a car?* These things do happen, not all the time, but they happen. Nevertheless, you shouldn't wait for something like that to occur before you make a decision. You might end up waiting the rest of your life and never buy a car at all, when you might really need one.

In thinking about the supernatural, we need to remember that we are forbidden to control it. That's why magic is forbidden. Magic is the control of the supernatural. Some churches try to get around this prohibition in subtle ways. For instance, some churches believe and practice that, after the band has warmed up and the singing is loud enough, the Holy Spirit will arrive. This is magic. The idea seems to be that the Holy Spirit will show up at 8:00, but not at 7:00, because the band is still warming up. It's only when we do our thing that the Holy Spirit will show up. This is not a good practice.

A Comprehensive Spirituality

Spirituality is not a part of our lives, but all of our lives. A comprehensive spirituality includes all the triangles we have considered: creativity, rationality, morality, emotions, language, relationships, body, and the supernatural.

Everything we do, except sin, is part of our spirituality. We should not see our lives as divided into the spiritual or supernatural versus the natural parts but integrated as a whole.

We don't understand all of this perfectly or see it all clearly. God has promised those who believe in Jesus that we will be completely restored to His intention for us. "Now we see as through a glass darkly, then we will see face to face. Now I know in part, then I shall know fully, even as I am fully known." (I Corinthians 13:12).

Smoked Glass

Purely beginning
Burning through various deaths
Our hearts turn to ice

Falsely beginning
Purified by Spirit's fire
Our hearts melt to flesh.

- a pair of Haiku by the author

32 Questions

1. What is hell?

Hell is part of the supernatural. God does not want death. God wants us to live. It's not God's will that any sinner should die, but that all will turn to Him, and live. In God's reality there is life, but not death. Death is a result of trying to live in another reality. So, although death actually happens, it isn't real. How does hell fit into this?

It seems to me that if we choose to consistently live outside of reality, the most likely thing that will happen is that we *unbecome*. The person in the Bible who spoke most about hell was Jesus. His word for hell was Gehenna. Gehenna was a real place. It was the garbage dump in the Kidron Valley, outside of Jerusalem. Gehenna was a good image because the garbage was burned, and the fire burned twenty-four hours a day. The flame didn't go out. The question, in terms of hell, is *What happens to the garbage?* We know the flame is eternal, but does the garbage burn eternally, or is the garbage burned up? Part of Jesus's message is that if we consider ourselves garbage, we will be garbage, and will go into the fire.

2. Another question is, Where does the fire come from?

It seems to me that it must come from God. Some people have a vague idea that the devil makes the fire, but I don't think the devil makes anything. The devil is not a creator. The devil is an accuser. The devil lives in unreality, in rebellion against God. He invites and entices other creatures to come and be with him, which is his way of consuming them. But the fire that we read about in the Bible comes from God. It is His glory. It is an eternal part of Him. The key issue, for us, is whether we encounter this fire as a *refining* fire versus a *consuming* fire. If we turn to God, and choose to live in His reality—if we want to be changed by Him—then we face the fire. It burns us and refines us, as silver being smelted in the crucible, as talked about in Malachai. The fire burns, and the impurities rise to the surface and are scraped off. The silver gets purer and purer; and the refiner is Jesus. He hovers over the boiling pot, and as the scum is scraped away, Jesus sees Himself in the silver, because we become more like Him as we are refined. However, if we don't turn to God, if we turn *away* from God, then the fire burns us from the back. The fire doesn't refine those who want to live in their own imagination, in their pride and vanity; it's the same fire, but it burns, consumes, and destroys. We know that the fire is eternal, because it's God, but again, the question is, is the garbage eternally burned or is the garbage burned up? It's a difficult question.

3. A related question is, Is hell eternally self-perpetuating, or would God have to sustain it forever?

Some people believe that God would, in fact, sustain such a parallel universe for eternity. It is a parallel universe, separate and apart, because it cannot exist within God's universe, which is truth and light, Spirit and love. This parallel universe is a false reality—proud, self-centered, destructive, and rebellious. Some would argue that God would not sustain such a separate universe, would not lend His creative power to keeping such a place in existence. In this case, since nothing can continue to exist without God's sustaining power, hell could not go on forever, but instead would fade away as those within it are burned up.

4. We sometimes hear that the left part of the brain is more sequential and linear in its processing, and the right part of the brain is more wholistic in its processing. Does the structure of the brain have any correspondence to time and eternity?

Probably not. The Bible tells us that we should have the mind of Christ, not the brain of Christ. The brain is a tool that the mind uses for thinking.

5. What is the mind?

We don't know entirely, but a passage that helps us understand the mind is from the Sermon on the Mount, where Jesus speaks of the eye being the lamp of the body. Jesus tells us when the eye is single, the body is full of light, but if the eye is evil, the body is full of darkness. When the eye is single, it sees everything in one focus and is undivided. The brain sees reality divided into linear and wholistic, but the mind is not divided unless it is evil.

6. How do we come to this singleness of mind?

By trusting God to do it for us. Trust corresponds to faith. I have faith that God will do to me and with me what is good and necessary. I make myself available to God working in me by trusting and obeying Him, so I am not totally passive. I choose to believe in God, I choose to trust Him, I choose to walk in the way that the Spirit indicates I should walk.

7. What should people do when this walk leads to pain and suffering?

We should accept the pain and suffering as growing pains. The last beatitude in the Sermon on the Mount is *Blessed are those who are persecuted for the sake of Jesus, for theirs is the kingdom of heaven.* When we follow Jesus, we are in two kingdoms, the kingdom of this world and the kingdom of heaven. There is a struggle and a battle. The stress and suffering of this battle are signs of life and membership in the kingdom of God.

8. Why do you think so many people associate being more spiritual with having transcendent or supernatural experiences?

One reason is that is seems to make spirituality easier. It is a kind of escape from full reality. People suffer in the natural world, and want the supernatural to be more real than the natural. People expect not to suffer in the supernatural part of reality. We are motivated to think this way by the devil, who wants to get us to see reality partly and not fully. Seeing reality fully means seeing it as both natural and supernatural.

9. If we see a vision, or have some other supernatural experience, that just comes to us, can we trust it?

We need to test our supernatural experiences and see if they belong to the Biblical truth as a whole. In I John 4:1-3, we are told to test our experiences to see if they acknowledge that Jesus Christ has come in the flesh. This means that the supernatural has become natural; the eternal has entered into time. Any vision or experience should not lead us away from this truth.

There's a story about Charles Spurgeon, a Baptist pastor in London. He was walking down the aisle of his church to preach in the pulpit. An angel of light stood in his way and said, "Charles Spurgeon, I have a message from the Lord for you." Spurgeon said, "I'm busy now, I'm about to preach." The angel said, "This is a very urgent message." Spurgeon said, "Okay, tell me." The angel said, "Your name is written in the Lamb's Book of Life." Spurgeon said, "The Bible has already told me that, and you are tempting me to believe the word of an angel. Go away." This is an example of testing the spirits. We are all different, and should not try to copy each other, but have the attitude of requiring clarity from a supernatural experience. The basic question, in various forms, is *Has Jesus Christ come in the flesh?* Spurgeon did not ask this question literally, but his concern was for Jesus Christ who is the Word of God, incarnated and written, to be the basis of his life.

10. Are there people who are more prone to an awareness of the supernatural? If so, what guidance would you give these people?

Some people, especially children, seem to be more aware of the supernatural than other people. My advice would be not to reject this awareness, but to be careful. If we emphasize the supernatural too much, we can come to believe that the supernatural is more real than the natural, which is not true. The belief that the supernatural is more real comes principally from the devil, but also through some philosophers like Plato. Christ-ism is not mysticism. Jesus is not only supernaturally real, but naturally real. The Word became flesh without becoming unspiritual.

11. Silence and stillness are often emphasized in non-Christian spiritual systems, especially meditative systems. Should silence and stillness play a role in the Christian life?

Yes, we should give space for listening to God, who speaks through his word, the Bible, and in other ways. We should be careful not to confuse silence and stillness with prayer, which is committed language.

12. If spiritual equals totally real, does spiritual also equal humility?

I wouldn't say that spiritual equals humility, but that humility is spiritual. Humility is basically realism, accepting who God is, what He does, and want He wants. When God called Moses at the burning bush to lead Israel, Moses said, *No, I am not qualified*. This was pride. Then, Moses accepted that God's will was right, which was humility. Moses was called the most humble man alive. He had the power of life and death over a million people, and he was humble.

13. What are the words the Bible uses to talk about spirituality?

When the Bible speaks of spirituality, it begins with God. It even says "God is Spirit". The words the Bible uses for spirit are ruah and pneuma, Hebrew and Greek words that both mean "wind". When the Bible says the Spirit blows where it wills, it says "The wind winds". The Spirit is expression or what goes out. A person has a spirit. So does a book or a song or a political party or a family or a church. They all express themselves and are active. The spirit expresses the whole person. It involves every part of the person. The fact of Jesus being the word of God through which everything was made shows us the creative effect of this wind or expression.

In the Gospel of John, 4:24, Jesus says "God is spirit". He doesn't say that God is spiritual or has spiritual parts. God is all spirit, so our understanding of what is spiritual is going to need to include all that we find out about God. Notice also that it doesn't work to say *Spirit is God*. If we think that way, then we end up starting with our experience of what we think spirit is and what we feel spirit is. We end up saying God is my understanding of spirit. It doesn't work because it begins with us. The same is true of love. If we want to know what love is, then we need to find out what is God-like. God is *love* is the correct equation. The false equation is love is God. Many people in our day, in post-modern times, believe in the false equation. They say My experience of love, or my assumptions or aspirations about love, are God. *If I know about these things then I'll know about God.* But I won't. I'll just know something about my insanity, about my own distortions. But if we say it the other way around—God is love—then we begin with God and can find out what love actually is. We need to let God define love in terms of Himself. The same is true of spirit. Everything we find out about God *is* spiritual, including the Incarnation.

14. Is technology spiritually evil?

New technologies in our world are starting to allow us to manipulate basic aspects of our being, whether through gene editing, creating interfaces between the brain and artificial intelligence, or other means. Should we be pursuing this? There should probably be some limits on these activities, although it may depend on how and why the technology is being used. Generally speaking, these technologies would be considered problematic and indeed evil if they were to, for instance, reduce or diminish basic aspects of our spirituality, reduce our ability to make choices, or reduce our ability to experience guilt and to see our need for forgiveness. So there should probably be limits, although we need to think and pray carefully to get an idea of the best way forward.

15. What were the consequences of the fall?

Death. By "death", I mean alienation and separation of things that God intends to be together. By "things" I mean, for example, one person and another person, people and God, and people from themselves, so that a person's body is separated from their mind and their spirit while alive to an extent, and then experiences a permanent separation when the body disintegrates. There is also an alienation of the human part of creation (human beings) from the non-human part of creation (plants, animals, rocks, streams, etc.). Death is unspiritual. Comprehensive spirituality, which is a gift of God through Jesus Christ, destroys death, and restores all of the relationship that God intends.

16. How can we live as fully human as possible in a fallen world?

Actively and passively. We allow God to live in us, and work in us for life, and we make choices to follow His guidance in His word (the Bible) and from the Holy Spirit who lives in us. All of the triangles need to be included in the choices that we make, so that we have a wholistic life and spirituality.

17. What is the difference between moral and ethical?

Moral means living within the absolute life guidelines of God. Immoral means living outside of those guidelines. Ethical means living within the temporary life guidelines of a culture. Unethical means living outside of those guidelines. People draw ethical lines. God draws moral lines.
If you have sex with someone who is not your spouse, you have crossed the line. But if you *think* about sex with someone who is not your spouse, you have also crossed the line.
We never are in the situation where we have not crossed the line. We are always sinners. We always need God's grace. We cannot keep ourselves safe.

18. Do scientists cross moral lines?

Scientists have always crossed the line into immorality. Ancient agronomical scientists discovered methods of intensive crop production, and destroyed the soil in the Tigris-Euphrates valley around 3000 or 4000 BC. Scientists have always taken what they discover out of the whole context of God's creation and been destructive. God wants people to explore His creation scientifically, but He wants us to take good care of creation with what we learn, and not just to impose a limited, egotistical manipulation on it that destroys it. So, when we begin to think about nano technology and things like that, the question remains the same as it was in ancient history. Science is mandated by God but it must be used responsibly and carefully in the whole context of God's creation, so that we don't reduce His creation and destroy it.

19. How can we tell if our church has become too rational in its interpretation of Scripture?

Even a little bit of rationality is wrong, if it is decontextualized from love. So if we think we can contain a vital and lively understanding in our minds, without living it out in love, we make a big mistake. Rationality is good and right, but it has to function within the context of love. If it becomes independent from love, it produces death. So the question is not *if* there is too much or too little rationality, but is the rationality practiced in the context of love?

There could be a church in a university town that has such a high level of rationality that the average person would feel alienated, but the rationality is practiced in the context of love, so there is no problem with it. On the other hand, there could be a church in a rural farming community, where nobody has ever been to college, and the rationality is practiced in a legalistic, egotistical, and exclusionary way; in this case, the rationality would be destructive.

20. Is it spiritual to take psychedelic substances to alleviate a psychiatric or medical condition?

I would think so, generally.

21. Is it spiritual to take psychedelic substances to come into contact with supernatural beings or realms?

We are required to test the spirits to see if they are from God. The test, as I mentioned earlier, is *Has Jesus Christ come in the flesh?* So, if a psychedelic drug gives us an experience that teaches us that the supernatural is more real than the natural, it is wrong (because Jesus Christ has come in the flesh and remained fully spiritual).

22. Can you give an example of the shalom of God in the context of suffering?

Shalom is well-being and security in God's truth and love. Shalom is a foundation and a framework for life that God provides. That foundation is equally effective whether we are happy or sad, or safe or in danger. It is not an absence of conflict, but a security within the conflict. The shalom of God is larger than the conflicts that we experience.

When I was hospitalized for depression, I was very, very sick, and in terrible pain. When I asked myself, "Am I safe in God's love?", the answer was always, "Oh yes, of course!"

23. Were there ever moments when you lost touch with this shalom?

There are moments when we all lose touch with it. It's a fallen world; we are all sinners. But in moments when we lose touch with God's shalom can be very happy or triumphant moments. When we are happy or triumphant, we can be tempted to become self-centered and to know good and evil in terms of our own experience and imagination, rather than in terms of God's truth. So I would say the happy, comfortable, and achieving moments of life are more dangerous than the moments of life that we do not enjoy. When we suffer, we tend to become more aware of our need of God. When we are triumphant or happy or comfortable, we tend to forget our need of God. To forget our need of God is to lose shalom. This corresponds to the first beatitude—blessed are the poor in spirit, for theirs is the kingdom of heaven—because it is only when we know that we need God that we have shalom.

24. How can we become more committed in our use of language?

Write down questions and statements, and come back to them after a day or two, and see if you would sign your name to them. Re-write until the questions and statements stabilize, and are the same every day. Some of my students have tried this, and it works. Others found it too hard and gave up. This exercise can be humiliating, because we may realize that we are chaotic and not committed to our speech. Although we can see that it would be possible to become more committed to our speech, the world around us encourages us in chaos. The people around us might say "Chill", "Loosen up", "Don't worry about it", "Just go with the flow", or "Whatever". Somebody once told me, "Don't become a wordsmith". To become more committed in the use of language is to be counter-cultural and anti-social in our present post-modern culture—and in this way, to become more spiritual.

25. Where does the human yearning for discovery and pattern-breaking come from?

God. God wanted to make creatures in His image. Human beings are in His image. The other creatures (animals) are not. Human beings are commanded by God to continue His process of creation by increasing the complexity of creation.

For instance, God made sheep and goats to wander in nature and follow the seasons. Human beings increase the complexity of sheep and goats by housing them in permanent and stable situations. What God does is called creation, and what people do is called art, because it's artificial.

26. What do people mean today when they say they are spiritual but not religious?

Largely, I don't know. So, if someone says that to me, I will ask them what they mean. Assuming that we know what another person means is often a great handicap to communication.

27. You said eternity is permanent and time is temporary. If time is temporary, then is it a distortion?

The creation as God made it was perfect. The relationship of time to eternity was perfect, without distortion. But sin and rebellion produced an alienation in reality that needs to be overcome by Jesus. The creation in time is an expression of the reality in eternity. God lives in eternity, before and outside the creation. Time and eternity are matrices of sequence. In space, things happen in time. Outside of space, things happen in eternity. There are various interfaces between time and eternity, the most important being revelation and prayer. When Jesus appears, everything will be brought together, into one matrix, and we will live in eternity.

28. How can we feel the working of the Holy Ghost?

We are filled with the Holy Spirit when we believe in Jesus. There is nothing in the Bible about how the Holy Spirit feels. At the same time, there is nothing in the Bible that tells us that the Holy Spirit doesn't feel like anything. But it doesn't tell us what we feel or how we feel.

29. What is a blessing?

A blessing is an enlargement of life—whereas a curse is a shrinking of life. We have generally a serious misconception that blessing feels good. Many blessings feel bad. The clearest example is the dentist. The dentist is a blessing. He feels bad. We're afraid of him. We avoid him. I think that's a symbol of all of life. The blessings very often feel bad, and the curses feel good. If you fall and break your leg on the street, and you're lying there in pain, and a doctor comes to you and says, "Oh, you poor dear, you must be in terrible pain, I see the bone sticking out of your skin, I will bless you"—and he injects you with morphine. In three seconds you feel wonderful. Then he says, "Now you are blessed," and he walks away. Are you blessed? No, you are cursed. Life is really confusing, and we need to look into the Bible and see what is blessing and what is cursing and to walk by faith.

30. What is heaven?

Heaven is the supernatural dimensions of reality. The dimensions of heaven are similar to, but different from, the dimensions of the natural reality. For instance, the natural reality functions basically in time, and the supernatural reality functions basically in eternity. Both time and eternity are matrices of sequence, which connect with each other. This means that every point of time is present to every point of eternity. At the end of temporal history, the prayer that Jesus taught us to pray, "Your kingdom come, Your will be done, on earth as it is in heaven", will be fully answered. The hope of Christianity is not that we will go to heaven, but that heaven will come to us. Time and eternity will conflate, and be one matrix of sequence. The separation between heaven and earth will end.

31. Sometimes people ask, "What will it be like to be in heaven?" Do you have any thoughts about this?

There are two stages or phases. One is to be with God after we die, but before the resurrection of the dead and the coming of heaven to earth. This is an in-between stage. The Bible indicates that people who die in the Lord will be with him, and know that they are with him, and also longing for their new resurrection bodies. The final reality is when heaven comes to earth, and heaven and earth are united, and we have our resurrection bodies. We have an example of a resurrection body in the resurrection of Jesus Christ. He ate and drank, and talked with people, and moved instantly through space and appeared physically in rooms without coming through the door or the window. So, the resurrection body will be similar to our natural body, and recognizable, but also different in ways that we do not fully know yet.

32. Why would we need a resurrection body that can eat and drink, since eating and drinking are associated with needing to give a physical body energy and to keep it alive?

It doesn't make any sense in terms of time and physical dimensions, but we will be in other dimensions, so it will make sense. However, we cannot understand this yet, from our current point of view. So the answer to the question is, *Wait and see.*

www.ingramcontent.com/pod-product-compliance
Lightning Source LLC
Chambersburg PA
CBHW070129080526
44586CB00015B/1624